Hand Gesture Recognition for Dumb and Blind Social Communication

Gestures communication between dumbs and other people using the expression of signs language an algorithm for recognizing hand gestures

---

By

Zahoor Mosaad Aydam

and

Assist. Prof. Dr. Shaker Kadhem Ali Al-Sharify

(Hand Gesture Recognition for dumb and blind Social Communication)

Copyright © 2009 by (Zahoor Mosaad Aydam And Assist. Prof. Dr. Shaker Kadhem Ali Al-Sharify)

ISBN (ISBN: 9798650996811
Imprint: Independently published)

Printed in USA by Amzon.cm)
Contact no. +9647814245592

mailto:Email:saviollamontella@yahoo.com

Dedication

To the of my father dear.

To the dearest person … my mother who provides me with love and compassion, I am still indebted for her.

To those whom a great source of support in my life … my brothers and sisters.

To everyone who taught me a single letter … my teachers whom I respect and grateful.

I dedicate this works …

zahoo

Foreword

Gestures are one of the best ways of communication between dumbs and other people using the expression of signs language. In this book, we suggest an algorithm for recognizing hand gestures of Arabic (letters or numbers or words) to by using dumb (through signs) and convert the sings into voice corresponding to sings (letters or numbers or words). The proposed algorithm use video for gesture of the dumb then convert the video into frames (images), preprocessing for the resulted image must done by remove the noise, resize the images and increase the contrast, then calculate the distance to clustering the words by using (C4.5 , k-mean , k- medoid and artificial neural network), calculate the distance (or features) by using Euclidean distance and slope where ,there are eighteen features (eight features from Euclidean distance, eight features from slop, Area, and perimeter). The results in the training stage were (C4.5 gave 99.8664% , k-mean gave 97.7930%,k-medoid gave 97.3620%and ANN gave 96.538%). While in the testing stage we used three classifiers (Euclidian Distance, Modify of the Standardize Euclidian Distance and Correlation) and the results show that (Euclidian Distance gave 94.7368%,Modify of the Standardize Euclidian Distance gave 98.2456% and Correlation gave 96.4912%) We create our database (ten videos with 814 frames..

Gestures communication between dumbs and other people using the expression of signs language an algorithm for recognizing hand gestures of (letters or numbers or words) to by using dumb (through signs) and convert the sings into voice corresponding to sings

preface

Communication is the method of trading musings, suppositions, data, or messages among the individuals by composing, discourse, or signs. Communication overcomes any barrier between individuals. There are various approaches to convey, where Communication is typically oral among individuals for example conversing with one another while moronic individuals can't speak with others as conventional individuals do. They can't talk, while the individuals who are hard of hearing can talk, yet incapable to hear and the visually impaired can't see however they can talk and hear the voice

Communication as correspondence by means of motions is the primary method of exchanging information between people. Conventionally motion used to speak with individuals when they would incline toward not to talk. This is the principle method of communication between a gathering of individuals who have poor hearing or can't talk. Correspondence dependent on motion is in like manner tongue does. Signals used by nearly the individuals communicate in various dialects, for example, American Sign Language (ASL) and Indian Sign Language (ISL). Correspondence might be through marking by utilizing hand movement either utilizing one hand or two hands. There are two sorts of signal based communication; confined and reliable motions. Single correspondence through marking contains single movement having single word, while constant ISL or consistent sign tongue is a plan of movements that make a noteworthy sentence the signs can be the movement by any part like face and hand. This movement of the hand might be the demonstration by recordings camera.

Acknowledgements

Praise to ((**Allah**)) the lord of majesty for His virtues and graces that He granted me and blessing and peace are upon the lord of creatures, the prophet of Allah Mohammed (**PBUT**) and his virtuous progeny.

One may fail to be grateful to those who have done favor, for neither polite words nor elegant sentences can be enough for such people. At the beginning, I must pay a due thank and gratitude to my respectable assistant professor (**Dr. Shaker Kadhim Ali Al-Sharify**), for supervising my thesis, granting me a due care and direction, and for the efforts he has made, as these efforts had a positive effect in producing this dissertation as best as possible. I owe him my gratitude and due thank. May Allah reward him for what he has done for me. May Allah make him a fund for learning and learned people.

My special thanks and deep gratitude to my professors at master, **Prof. Dr. Kadhim M. Hashim,Dr. Khaldun I. Arif, Dr. Kadhim H. K. Alibraheemi, Dr. Hazim B. Tahir, Dr. Mustafa J. Hayawi , for their support and encouragement throughout my study.**

And as fulfillment for people with gratitude and appreciation to the owners of the generosity. I express my sincere thanks and appreciation and great gratitude to most respectable (**Mr. Amer Mahdi Yaseen and Dr.Ahmed Abdul Hussein Ouda).**

There have been many more people involved in this thesis, whose names may not have been mentioned above, but their help is undoubtedly acknowledged, I thank them all.

Abstract

Social communication is the means of expressing opinions or ideas through verbal or nonverbal communication. Verbal communication between ordinary people through speaking. Dumb people who cannot speak are communicating with people who can speak through nonverbal communication through gestures. The blind person who cannot see but can hear they can communicate with people by talking to them. In this thesis, an Algorithm was proposed to communicate between the dumb person and the blind person by a gesture for the dumb person and convert it into a voice to communicate with dumb (through the signals) where the blind hearing the voice that converted from. This is because gestures are one of the best ways to communicate between the dumb and the blind through the use of sign language, which is transformed into a voice that the blind can hear and communicate with each other.

The proposed Algorithm consist of two parts : training and testing .Each type of Algorithm includes different stages ; acquisition , preprocessing ,segmentation ,features extraction and classify. The first stage is the acquisition of video or images where the video must be convert into images (frames) and then image pre-processing stage by converting images into gray level then into binary images and apply morphology operation, the resulted image will be as mask for segmentation stage by multiply the mask by the original image (gray scale image) the resulted image will be rotated and convert into binary image again and use it as mask to multiply by rotated image then fixed the size of images and convert the resulted image into binary image. The features extraction stage evaluates features from the resulted image by computing the geometry features (18 features). Then will be classify by using one of clustering Algorithms and classification Algorithms (K-means, K-medoid, C4.5, ANN) and build database for testing, while in testing part we do the same steps in first part without using clustering Algorithms , the   classification will be using three metrics ways (Euclidean distance, Modify of the Standardized Euclidean distance and correlation).

The results from using four Algorithms were ; K-means gives 97.7930%, k-medoid gives 97.3620%, C4.5 gives 99.8664% and ANN gives 96.5386%. while in testing part we got the following results; Modify of the standardized Euclidean distance gives(98.2456% & 3ms), for correlation efficiency gives(96.4912% & 4ms)and Euclidean distance gives(94.7368% & 2ms) .

List of Contents

List of Figures

List of Tables

List of Abbreviations

Abbreviation	Meaning
ISL	Indian Sign Language
ASL	American Sign Language
DTW	Dynamic Time Warping
ArSL	Arabic Sign Language
ANFIS	Adaptive Neuron -Fuzzy Inference System
KNN	k-nearest neighbour
DLLE	distributing locally linear embedding
PNN	probabilistic neural network
FD	Fourier Descriptor
OH	Orientation Histogram
PCA	Principal Component Analysis
PSL	Pakistani Sign Language
DWT	Discrete Wavelet Transform
HMMs	Hidden Markov Models
ANN	Artificial neural network
RNNs	Recurrent neural networks
MLP	Multi-layer perceptron

List of Algorithms

CHAPTER ONE
GENERAL INTRODUCTION

Chapter one
General Introduction

1.1 Introduction

Communication is the way of exchanging thoughts, opinions, information, or messages among the people by writing, speech, or signs. Communication bridges the gap between the people. There are different ways to communicate, where communication is usually oral among people i.e. talking to each other while dumb people cannot communicate with others as ordinary people do. They cannot speak, while the people who are deaf are able to speak, but unable to hear and the blind are unable to see but they can speak and hear the voice [1].

Communication via gestures is the main way of trading data between individuals. Ordinarily gesture used to communicate with people when they would prefer not to talk.   This is the main way of communication between a group of people who have poor hearing or are unable to speak. Communication-based on gesture is likewise dialect does. Gestures utilized by almost the people they speak different languages such as American Sign Language (ASL) and Indian Sign Language (ISL). Communication may be through signing by using hand motion either using one hand or two hands. There are two types of gesture-based communication; isolated and consistent gesture. Single communication through signing comprises of single motion having one word, while continuous ISL or continuous sign dialect is an arrangement of motions that create a significant sentence the signals can be the motion by any part like face and hand. This motion of hand may be the act by videos camera[2].

Gesture recognition technique basically consists of two classes: data computer vision-based approach and gloves-based approach. The first one has used processing video images and distinguish patterns for hand gesture recognition and interaction. The second one depends on the hardware and gets information from the hand joints through of sensors that to receive a hand gesture classification[3].

Gesture recognition uses many input devices, such as color cameras, information gloves, a Microsoft Kinect sensor, departure time, etc. Although the data glove-based gesture recognition systems have achieved good performance than other systems, data gloves are so expensive and not comfortable to use, which limits their popularity[4].

Gesture recognition systems may be applied as a normal , intuitive , suitable way for the react between computational systems and human beings. These systems use human movement patterns to recognize, impart, and propagate gestures carried out by a use. There are many applications of recognizing gestures; such as games, human-robot interaction, interaction with televisions. The way in which the signal is distinguished at the present by the capture of human gestures using only a video camera on a smartphone or tablet or laptop[5].

We proposed an Algorithm to help the dumb and blind to communicate effectively with each other by taking video from the dumb person and converting it into images (frames) where each image contains a sign indicating one of the(letters ,a number ,or a word)and then a recognizing each letter, number or word into voice to help blind people .

1.2 Gestures

Gestures are the physical movement that reinforces the verbal message and carries precise ideas or feelings. The gesture can be used with the head, shoulders, legs or feet, mostly in the hands and arms. Gestures are types of nonverbal physical communication that do no longer send precise messages, like pure, close, and frequent expressions [6]. Gestures communicate a variety of thoughts and feelings, starting with hatred then quarrel according to vindication or affection, and often the gestures are the body language and words when they speak [7].

1.2.1 Why Gestures?

Gestures are the most nonverbal means of communication in terms of the effects that a speaker can perform. There is no other type of physical movement that can enhance speech the same way gestures do. Gestures may use for [8]:

1. **Explaining and supporting your own:** Gestures help your audience to get a better understanding of your verbal message.
2. **Expressing your thoughts:** When you match gestures to what you say, they help draw a vivid picture in the minds of your audience.

3. **Bringing vitality and focus on the words of the speaker:** They could depict feeling in a more clear way than words.

4. **Helping overcome nervous tension:** Targeted gestures is a better vent for the nerve energy generated in the speaking position.

5. **Working as visual aids:** The gestures enhance public attention and memory.

6. **Motivating public participation:** Gestures help you get the reaction you want from the audience.

7. **Clarifying vision:** Gestures provide visibility support in the case of addressing a large number of people and the public as a whole cannot see your eye

1.2.2 Types of Gestures

Regardless of a large number of gestures, all of them can mainly belong to one of the following groups[9]:

1. **Meta gestures:** Illustrate and reinforce the verbal message and help the public to get accurate comparisons and visualize shape, size, location, movement and function and the number of objects as well.

2. **Confirmation gestures:** They refer to seriousness, for instance, the first offers a powerful feeling, such as anger or insistence.

3. **Proactive gestures are key to thoughts and feelings:** Which help the speaker to make the desired mood or to show a certain idea. The open hand refers to the presentation or reception of an idea while shrugging shoulders indifferently refers to ignorance, puzzlement or ridicule.

4. **Inductive gestures:** They use to induce the desired reaction of the public. If you try to persuade the audience to raise their hand's dap or

do any movement, you will enhance the possibility of a reaction if you do an example yourself.

1.3 Literature Review

Symeonidis [10] offered hand gesture recognition mode employ neural networks to recognize constant hand gestures, namely, it is the subset of American Sign Language (ASL). He utilizes McConnel's concept of Orientation Histograms in conjugation together with neural networks and for few of edge revelation technicalities. Its systems employ data gloves or signs to enter into the system.

Tang [11] suggest mode to extraction the orders of gestures; gesture discovery and recognition for actual-time music execution. The main aim of structuring a gesture recognizer is to employ it in actual-time rendering. Through traineeship, a single little gesture vocabulary prior to the execution, musicians mastery employ the gesture recognizer to forward they instructions for the computer .So, musicians· ability to control voice parameters or output voices without the help of offstage voice engineers. He utilizes a gesture threshold sample for a Dynamic Time Warping (DTW) Algorithm in order to detect and classify gestures. The system send-off recognized orders by OSC messages. He presently backing Microsoft Kinect and wireless sensor on the body as input.

Al-Jarrah [12] developed a system of the automatic translation to gestures of the hand alphabet in the Arabic Sign Language(ArSL).They were set up a group of Adaptive Neuron-Fuzzy Inference System (ANFIS) networks, every of whose is training to identify one gesture. The system do not utilize any gloves or optical signs to perform the job of recognition.

Rather than, transact with bare hands images, who permits the user to react for the system in a normal. The subtractive clustering Algorithm and the less squares to determine a fuzzy inference system, training is performed utilizing the hybrid education Algorithm. That system identifies the 30 Arabic Sign Language alphabets visually, it utilizing bare hand images.

Youssef [13] suggest an automatic identification system of Arabic sign language founded on the Hidden Markov Models. A great collection of specimens has been utilized to recognition 20 secluded words of the regular Arabic sign language. That system is signer-separate. Experiences are conducted employ real ArSL videos pick it up for deaf people at various clothing and for various colors. Plain classify techniques like k-nearest neighbour (KNN), linear and Bayesian were utilize. Their utilize database composed of a 20-word, the database herself composed of 45 duplications of every one of the 20 words complete by means of various signers, the stocked videos is be saved in the AVI style.

Ge [14] offered an unsupervised education Algorithm, interested the problem of dynamic gesture pursuit, distributing locally linear embedding (DLLE) and continual hand gesture recognition Which has been developed to discover the essential build of the data, like perform images in a minimal dimensional space and neighbourhood relations information. They used a probabilistic neural network (PNN) and they employ database include the group of constant gesture classification.

The neighborhood preserving feature of DLLE protected the adjacent relation of the movement series images in weakened -dimensional space. They made employ of the likeness measures between the images, in which

hand gesture movement from a series of images mastery be follow up and build it dynamically according to for the relative position of images in the conformable movement database.

Chen [15] suggested a hand gesture recognition system utilizing a genuine-time pursuant mode and Hidden Markov Models to recognition 20 various continual gesture before constant background. Theirs apply a genuine-time hand pursuance and extraction Algorithm to tracing hand movement and extractor the hand area, thereafter their utilize the Fourier Descriptor (FD) to describe Spatial characteristics and the movement analysis to features the temporal features. They pool the temporal and spatial characteristics of the enter image series as our own feature vector. Next, to have extracted the advantage vectors, the Hidden Makarov Models Algorithm is applied to identify the input gesture.

Shroffe [16] suggested the way for extraction of various hand gestures based EMG signal utilize artificial neural network in developing the human-computer interface that helps disabled people react for computers.

The EMG styles are extracted of the signals at every motion and the characteristics (such as average absolute worth, root medium square, contrast, the criterion deviation, middle frequency, zero intersection and slope signal variation) extracted of the signal are offered to a neural network for traineeship and the rating.

Chen [17] offered a genuine- time hand gesture recognition utilizing finger fragmented. In the frame, the hand area is extracted from the background with the way to subtract background. The hand and fingers are fragmented. For, detection the fingers in the hand image and identify them, they used HSV pattern to hand color area discovery of another motion object. Learn about motion hand by simple rule workbook.

Tripathi [2] offered recognize system for gesture in Indian Sign Language using both hands to perform any namely gesture. It represents the identification of gestures the sign language of persistent gestures be a big challenge to solve this problem by taking advantage of the hierarchy of an open frame list. It is a useful framework for segmenting continuous sign language movements into signal chains and also for removing the unnecessary frame. After division, each gesture is treated as a secluded gesture. Next to that, The features are then extracted before processing by utilizing Orientation Histogram (OH) with Principal Component Analysis (PCA) is applied for a To reduce in the dimension of features acquired after OH . They use different types of classifiers such as correlation , Euclidean distance, distance Manhattan, etc. The rating efficiency is measured here by the maximum number of frames are identical. Experiment results show The designed way gives good results with Euclidean distance and correlation.

Liu Yun [18] offered the way recognize the hand gesture on the basis of multi-feature merge and template matching this way reveals the contour area in the form of a hand and gets the biggest contour according to the skin color property, by extraction number of angles and angle skin color, and the color angle not related to the skin in along with fixed moments features from the biggest hand-shaped region to specimen training. The Euclidean distance template matching is employed for hand gesture recognizing and classification. Results showed this the way does good as to extract the various hand gestures features and to identify the cascading matching template using accurate Euclidean distance classification.

Kausar [19] offered a fuzzy matrix to identify the alphabets of the suggested Pakistani sign language(PSL). In the suggested way, varicolored gloves are utilized to select every finger-tip and joint. Calculate the angle between the tip of the finger and the finger joint symmetric and utilized to determine the position of every finger and then that positions are utilized to recognize the sign language alphabet. Angles are supplied as input to the fuzzy inference system the system then determines the position of every finger and based on these positions the operation defuzzification is performed. The results showed that the precision of the suggested system is very high; only two signs out of thirty-seven cannot be recognized through the system properly; every another 35 signs it was recognized strictly.

Suresh [20] presented an effective ISL recognition system is the suggested the ISL recognition system is a technique for identifying patterns that contain two important units: feature extraction and classification. Employ Otsu thresholding and morphological processes are utilized for the segmentation execution. DWT is implementation up to the 7th level for calculating sub-band power features In order to get the best set of features. It has been shown that the nearest neighbour plant used for classification provides a %99.23 precision when using a cosine metric.

Kumar [21] showed gesture recognize utilize Hidden Markov Models Enhanced using the effective expectations of the activities of a new way to recognition time-changing human gestures of continued video

current. They suggested ways reveal skeleton joint information into Hidden Markov Models provided together with active variance signatures to check segmentation to identify the latest technologies . The suggested way on the comfort tires or the subject site in the special gesture segmentation. The method benefit is determined by two sets of data that are widely utilized in gesture research: 1) ChaLearn, a continuous gesture dataset, and 2) MSR3D, an isolated gesture dataset.

Foong [22] presented hand gesture recognition: log in to the audio system a system as a model that is capable to automatic identification of sign language to assist ordinary people to communicate more efficacy together with people who are hearing impaired or who have impaired speech. The audio system a system as a model, S2V, was a development of the system using the feed forward neural network nerve for cascading signals. Various collections of global hand gestures were caught on the video camera and used to traineeship the neural network for rating objective. The experimental results showed that the neural network achieved a satisfactory result of the translation into sound.

Elmezain [23] viewed hand gestures recognition based to merged features to extract recognition a system on numbers (0-9) and alphabetical characters (A-Z) in actual - time of stereoscopic image sequences utilizing Hidden Markov Models (HMMs). Their system is founded on third prime phases; automatic partitioning and pre-processing of hand areas, extract features and classify them in the automatic partitioning phase, color, and 3D profundity map are utilized for hand discloser where the hand path will occur will in another step utilizing a Mean-shift Algorithm and Kalman filter. In the feature extraction phase, the built-in 3D features of the site are used with speed and oriented while respecting Cartesian system. And then is used, k-means clustering and HMMs code word. In the final phase, the classification is called uses the Baum-Welch Algorithm is used to make a complete train for HMMs parameters. The letters and numbers are recognized using a pattern Left-Right Banded in conjugation together with the Viterbi Algorithm. The experimental results show that the system can recognize the hand gesture successfully by 98.33%.

Wong [24] viewed persistent gesture recognition utilizing a Sparse Bayesian classifying way to recognize and split 9 initial gestures from the video input . The proposed application can be recognized for continuous labeling. A secluded gesture is recognized using the first convert part of the video to a movement gradient direction image and then classified into a unity of gestures 9 gestures by means of a sparse Bayesian classifier. The part of the video utilized is technical sampling based on frame condensation. Through act so, gestures may be split form video in a probability manner.

A way can check accuracy 90% in recognition of gestures secluded and continuous without the use of private gear like glove devices and ability turn on the system in genuine time.

1.4 Research problem

According to the statistics provided by the World Health Organization, there are 285 million people around the world suffer from blindness, one million are dumbed and many suffer from other physical disabilities . Human life is easier and more convenient within a short period of time. The advances in science and technology have attained a great level in making the communication system between the dumb and the blind. We have encountered many techniques that have made our lives much easier and more convenient, within a few decades [25].

People with physical disabilities need to feel that they are also part of society and can also go along with others .There are few means of communication between people such as braille to communicate between the blinds, and gestures as the most common way to communicate between the dumb and the blind [1].

The problem is how to help people with physical disabilities to communicate easily with each other (dumb and blind). This research focuses on the above problem and attempts to develop a new Algorithm that enables the dumb and the blind to communicate with each other by referring to the dumb person and breaking the gap.

1.5 Aims and Objectives

The main goal of this thesis is to suggest a new Algorithm for communication between the dumb and the blind by using dumb sing (as video) and convert the video into images (frames) then classify each word, letters or number into voice to make the blind hear the words, letters or numbers.

1.6 Thesis Organization

In addition to this chapter the thesis consists of other four chapters; they are:

Chapter Two: In this chapter, we will explain the theoretical background of our suggested Algorithm.

Chapter Three: This chapter shows the design and implementation steps of the proposed Algorithm.

Chapter Four: This chapter contains the main datasets used. The test results are presented and discussed to evaluate the performance of the established Algorithm.

Chapter Five: This chapter contains some conclusions and a list of future work.

CHAPTER TWO
THEORETICAL
BACKGROUND

Chapter two
Theoretical background

2.1 Introduction

The theoretical background of the proposed Algorithm is divided into four types of clustering Algorithms; K-mean, K-medoid, Neural network and C4.5 also we need to explain the feature extraction of Geometric methods such as Euclidian distance, Slop, Angle, Area, Perimeter, Rotation, centroid and Points extrema features.

2.2   Clustering

Cluster analysis or clustering is the task of grouping a set of objects in such a way that objects in the same group (called a cluster) are more similar (in some sense) to each other than to those in other groups (clusters)[26]. The conception of data collecting is evident and close to human in its way of thinking. As shown in Figure(2.1).

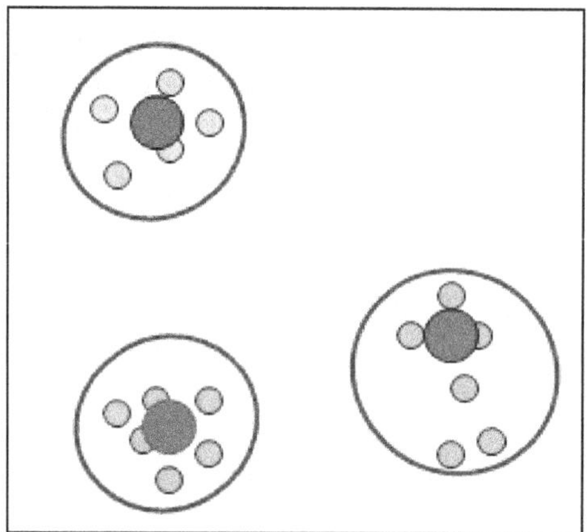

Figure (2.1): data clustering

It is a main task of exploratory data mining, and a common technique for statistical data analysis, used in many fields, including machine learning, pattern recognition, image analysis, information retrieval, bioinformatics, data compression, and computer graphics[27].

2.2.1 Definition and Terminology

The followings are some of the definitions that are proposed to define data clustering [28].

Let 'X' be the data set defined as

$$S = \{X_1, X_2, \dots X_m\} \tag{2}$$

The partition of S into m sets (clusters): $P_{i},\dots\dots,P_m$ is defined as an m-clustering of S, So that the following conditions are met:

$$Pi \neq \phi, i = 1 \dots m \tag{2}$$

$$U_{i=1}^{m} P_i = S \tag{2}$$

$$Pi \cap Pj = \phi, i \neq j, j = 1, \dots, m \tag{2}$$

equations (2.2), (2.3) and (2.4) shows the vectors in group Si have more similarity with each other and at the same time differ from other groups. This similarity has been addressed through different measures as long as different data from different types of clusters.

The development of the clustering task, we have to follow some of the required stages[29,30]:

1. Clustering Algorithms.

2. Geometric features

3. Measurement similarity.

2.2.2 Clustering Algorithms

There are many of different Algorithms can be used for clustering; these Algorithms can be classified according to the method of data entry to the Algorithm, and the assembly criteria that determine the similarity between the data points and the theory and the basic concepts underlying the clustering techniques[31]. These Algorithms can be classified as follows:

1. Partition clustering attempts to analyze data directly into a group of disjoint clusters. More specifically, they try to identify an integer of sections to improve the function of a given standard. The function of the standard may emphasize and improve the local or global data structure [31]. Typical methods: k-means, k-medoids.

2. Hierarchical is prepared around the thought of identical objects with a nearer distance that is more attached to each other than distant objects. Can be split into two approximation methods; aggregation methods, where the subjects begin in a separate own set. Then the next two groups (the most similar) are combined and repeated over and over until all subjects are in one group. Finally, the optimal number of clusters is selected from all clustering solutions, divisive clusters that begin with one set for the entire data set and are frequently divided minimal the hierarchy. In general, the consequence of a hierarchical

aggregation Algorithm is a diagram illustrating the composition of clustering [32].

3. Density-based data sets collect data points based on the locating of intensive clusters of points. so, data points in higher intensity areas end over in itself group[33].

4. Grid-based ways create the point space (object) in a given number of cells that make up a network structure. whole groups are performed on the network structure (that is, in the quantity area). The prime feature of such process is speedy handling time, where it is generally freelance from the number of data points while relying only upon the number of cells at every distance on the quantity area [31].

2.2.2.1 K-means cluster

K-means is the most popular   diffusion partitioning style. This Algorithm was suggested by Mac-Queen in 1967. K-mean is a not sequent, unspecified, repetitive mode of gathering. At k-mean, every block is shown resented by means of the medium value of the things at the set. we split a set of object n into the set of k in which the cluster parity is low and the inter-cluster like is high. Measurement of similarity by the middle worth of objects in a group[34].This Algorithm is used to cluster several data depending on their properties to the K clustering, and the assembly process is done by reducing the distances between the data and the cluster center[35].The Figure(2.2) shows the K-Means Clustering Algorithm.

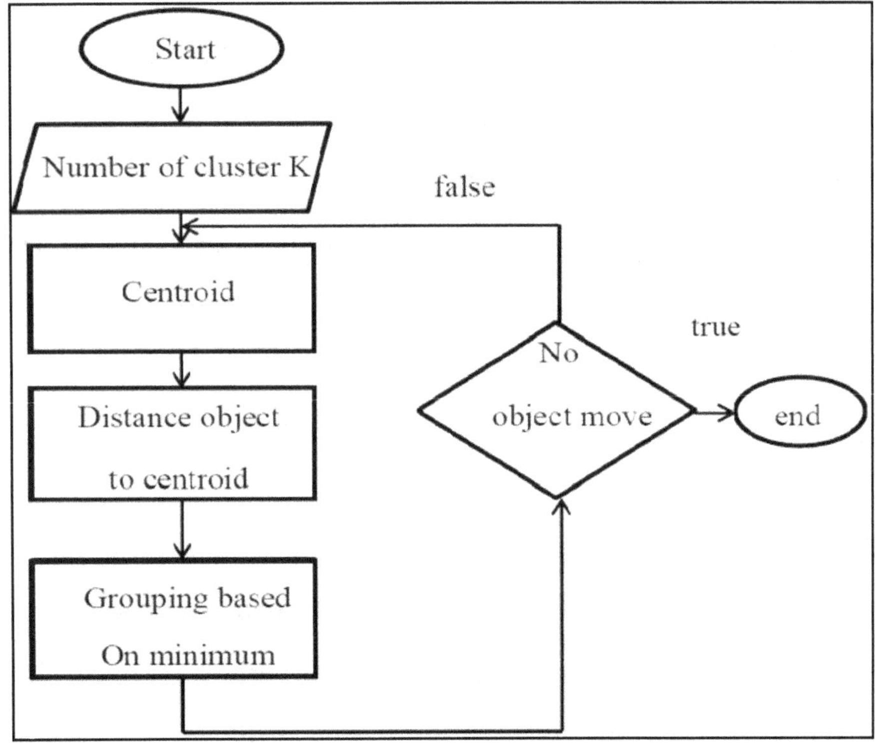

Figure (2.2): K-means

Figure (2.2): K-mean Algorithm

2.2.2.2   K-medoid cluster

K-Medoids clustering is one of the clustering Algorithms. Instead of using the mean and central, K-Medoids clustering is one of the non-automatic clustering Algorithms. Instead of employing classical centroid, it

is used medoids to characterize the clusters. The medoid is a statistic step, which appears that the data member of a dataset whom medium disagreement into another member of the group is minimized. so, a medoid, different medium, it is ever a member of the data group. It represents the most centralized object data object in the data group.

The action of the K - Medoids Algorithm is like to K-Means clustering Algorithm. It also starts with at randomly chosen k data provision as primary medoids to configure the k clusters. All of the other remaining elements consisted   in a cluster, which possesses its medoid relative to elements. A new medoid is chosen, that can represent the best class .The whole remaining data items are once location assigned to the cluster having closer medoid. Repetition, medoids alteration ,their location, the Algorithm minify the aggregate of the divergences inter every data element and its conformed medoid. Repeat this cycle even if Medoid does not change its location.

This indicates the end of the operation while the result of final clusters together with their medoids are defined. K clusters, which are centered on the medoids ,are formed, and each of the data members is laid down on the suitable clustering founded on closest medoid [36].

2.3 Classification

Classification is a method to extract the data and the division of this data into categories or specific groups in advance. It is a way to learn under the supervision of training requires disaggregated data to induce rules for the classification of categorizing data. There are two phases; the first stage is the stage of learning, which training data analysis and creating classification rules. The second stage is a classification, where the test data is classified into categories based on the rules generated [37]. There are two classification Algorithms in this thesis. Such as the C4.5 Algorithm and ANN.

2.3.1 C4.5 Algorithm

C4.5 is a most important Algorithm used for decision making and creating decision trees. It is one of developments of the ID3 Algorithm used to overcome its flaws. Decision maker " decision trees" created by the C4.5 Algorithm can also be used for classification. It turns out that C4.5 is also regarded as a statistical classifier. It produces a number of change to upgrade the ID3 Algorithm[38]. Some of these changes are mentioned [37].

Dealing with training data with missing values for attributes that deal with different cost characteristics in pruning decision tree after their characteristics in dealing with both kinds of values :discrete and continuous.

Consider a training data set of $X = x_1, x_2 \ldots x_n$ of the already sorted samples. Each sample is $Xi = s_1$ and $s_2 .. s_n$. Is a vector where s_1 and $s_2 .. s_n$ represent the attributes or features of the sample. Data is simply a vector $D = d_1$ and $d_2 .. d_n$ where d_1 and $d_2 .. d_n$ represent the class to which each sample belongs.

In each node of the tree, C4.5 chooses one attribute for data that divides the data set from X more effectively into subsets that can be one class or another. Is the natural gain of information (the difference in entropy) that results from the choice of a feature to divide the data. The attribute factor is considered with higher gain normalized information for decision making. The C4.5 Algorithm then keeps processing on the smaller sub-lists that have the maximum natural gain of information [39].

A. Entropy

Assume the probabilities $P_1, P_1, \ldots, P_s$, where $\Sigma P_i = 1$, Entropy is defined as follows:

$$I(s_1, s_2, \ldots \ldots, s_m) = \sum - (P_i \log_2 P_i) \qquad (2.5)$$

Where P_i is the probability that a sample in S_j belongs to class C_i

.Entropy finds the amount of the request in a specific database state. The value of H = 0 is a fully classified group. So that, the higher of the entropy, the greater the possibility of improving taxonomy [40].

B. Gain information G (D, S)

C4.5 chooses the splitting attribute with the highest gain in information similar ID3 , where gain is defined as difference between how much information is needed after the split. This is calculated by determining the differences between the entropies of the original dataset and the weighted sum of the entropies from each of the subdivided datasets. The formula used for this purpose is[41]:

It defines the gain for a test S and a position D

$$G(D,S) = H(D) - \sum P(D_i)H(D_i) \tag{2.6}$$

where values (D_i) is the set of all possible values for attribute S.

C. Gain ratio

It differs from information gain, which measures the information with respect to classification that is acquired based on the same partitioning.The gain ratio is defined as

$$Gain\ Ratio(D,S) = G(D,S)/Split\ Info(D,S) \tag{2.7}$$
Where

$$Splitinfo(D,S) =- \Sigma\ (|Dj|/|D|) * log\ ((|Dj|/|D|)) \tag{2.8}$$

D =data Set, S=Sub attribute from attribute, $(|Dj|/|D|)$=act as weight of jth partition.

The attribute with the maximum gain ratio is selected as the splitting attribute. Note , however, that as the split information approaches 0, the ratio becomes unstable. A constraint is added to avoid this, whereby the

information gain of the test selected must be large-at least as great as the average gain over all tests examined [42].

2.3.2 The Artificial Neural Network

ANNs are computer models based on mathematical models that, unlike classical computing, have a structure and operation comparable to those of the human brains. ANNs are called connectivity systems, distributed or adaptive systems, because of their consists of a chain of interrelated handling elements that work at the same time.

One of the authentic objectives of artificial neural networks was to understand and form the functional features and computational particulars of the brain in conducting cognitive operations like as sensory perception, classification of concepts, a collection of concepts and learning. Today, however, a major effort is being made to develop neural networks for implementations like as style recognition, classify data pressure and optimization[43].

2.3.2.1 Main Architectures of Artificial Neural Networks

In generically, an artificial neural network can exist split into three parts, termed layers, as following [44]:

A. Input layer

This layer is receiving data, signs, properties, or gauges from the exterior environment. Those inputs (samples or styles) are generally normalized within the border values resulted by activation functions. This

\normalization consequence in best numerical accuracy for the mathematical operations by the network.

B. Hidden Layers

This layer is composed of neural cells which are responsible for extracting styles linked with the operation or system being the test. This layer fulfills most of the inside treatment of a network.

C. Output layer

This layer also consists of neural cells, and it is responsible for the product and display the definitive network produce, who result from handling by neural cells in former layers. The fundamental architecture of ANN can be divided, taking into account the order of neurons, how they are interconnected and how their layers are formed, as follows:

2.3.2.1.1 Feed forward networks

Feed forward   networks include Single-layer feeding networks ,routing networks   and multilayer feeding networks as following:

A. Single-layer feeding networks

This network is the simple type of neural networks consisting of one input layer and one output layer of processing units. There are no rear feed connections. This network is called a monolayer network, with a label monolayer   that refers to the output layer in the contract of the account (neurons). We do not count the input layer to hold the source because there is no account here [45]. As shown in Figure (2.3).

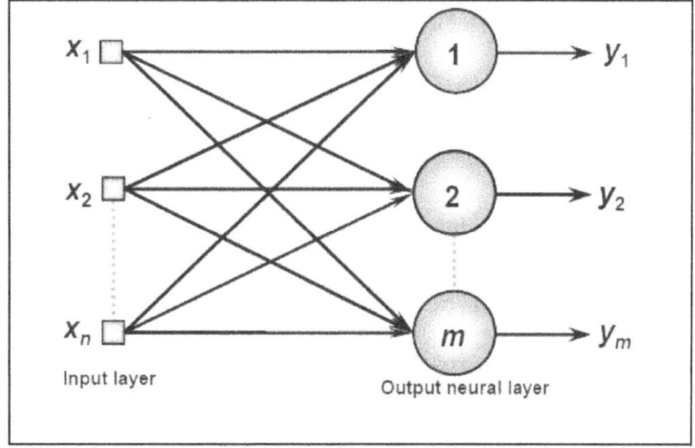

Figure(2.3): feed forward for single layer

B. Multilayer feeding networks

Multi-layer   network differs from the previous network, as it contains one   or more layers called (hidden layers) as well as the input layer and the output layer where the output of each hidden layer is an entry to the next layer and so on for each layer in this network which considered as a single layer network . The class that gives the output is called the output layer, the input layer is not considered a layer, and the rest of the layers are called the hidden layers. Figure (2.4) shows the network for one hidden layer [46] .

This network is distinguished by its ability to solve more complex problems than those that can be solved in single-layer networks because of the presence of hidden layers that give greater flexibility in the construction of functions between inputs and outputs Although the training of these networks takes long time, but the training of these networks is more successful than others which can be caused a problem cannot be solved at all by using a single-layer network even if trained for a long time and many problems require the use of multilayered networks to resolve and the distinguishing features of the problem are to determine the type of networks that are to be used.

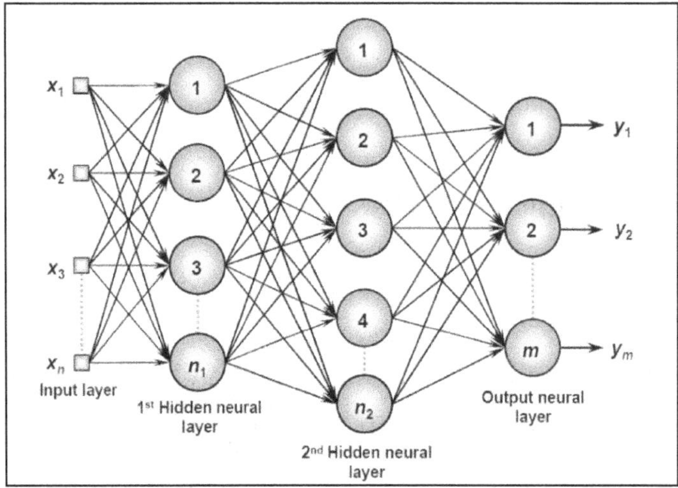

Figure (2.4): Multilayer feed forward network

2.3.2.1.2 Recurrent networks (RNNs)

Recurrent neural networks layers can change weights in both directions through the relationships within the network .The output of each layer can be input into the previous layers or input into the same layer. Recurrent neural networks are very powerful and complex, which are dynamic networks whose stability change constantly until reaching the balance Recurrent neural networks are one of the nonlinear methods used in predicting time series, identification , patterns recognition and classes .It is described as a dynamic system [45].Figure (2.5) shows an example of repeated neural networks.

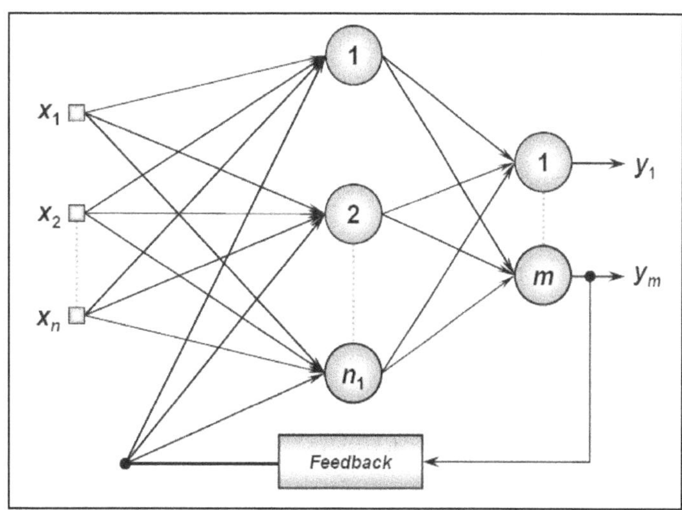

Figure (2.5): Recurrent network together with a hidden layer

In general, neural network training ability is classified into three master sets: supervised learning, unsupervised learning and reinforcement learning [47]. Theses use multi-layered neural networks.

2.3.2.2 Basic Principles of Learning in Neural Networks MLP

Neurons connect to a network so that being the output of every neuron is an input to single or more another neuron. The communication can be between neurons either single- directional or multi-directional, and according to intensity the communication can be exciting or inhibitory. Neurons are arranged into layers. There are two main types of layers: the hidden layers and output layers [47,48].

The hidden layer is the arithmetic nodes can be named as hidden neurons or hidden unities . The expression hidden reference to the reality that this section of the neural network is not fair visible such as the input or output of the network. The function of hidden neurons is to interfere between outer inputs and to take out the network in a helpful way. Through add to one or many hidden layers, the grid is can to extract the higher arrange statistics from them inputs. In a fair meaning, the network gains a universal perspective although its domestic connection, because of the additional collection of synaptic connections as well as the extra dimension of neural interactions and the output layer, the class responsible for producing and displaying network outputs [45].

In this meaning, the training process takes the data to the input layer of the network, where each input is multiplied by the connection weight. The first layer is the input layer and the input units divide the inputs on the blocks into the next layers[48].

By providing elements such as the activation style (input vector), the output of neuron calculated on basis of conversion function, noting that the activation function, may be a linear or non-linear function to enter. The transfer function is selected according to the type of issue that wants to be resolved through the network. More common activation functions are: the important zigzag function, threshold function, linear function, x-function, which is input signs used to neurons in the second layer (i.e first hidden layer) and the second layer will be input signs used to neurons of the third layer, and so on for the reminded of network. Usually, neurons in every layer of a network layer have input-output signs for the former layer only. The array of output signals for neurons in the output layer of the network establishes the total response of the network to the activation pattern provided through the nodes exporter in the input layer (the first) [45].

The architectural graph in Figure (2.6) shows the multi-layered feed forward multi-layer neural network

x_i(n): Network input

f_j and f_k: the output of hidden layers

(Y_l) n: network output.

w_{ij}, w_{jk}, and w_{kl}: connected weights between the input and the first hidden layer and, the weights connected between the first hidden layer and the second hidden layer, the weights connected between the second hidden layer and the output layer respectively.

m: is the number of neurons in the first hidden layer.

Each of the output elements from the first hidden layer can be calculated according to the following equation [49].

$$W \qquad \sum^{q} b_j + x_i w_{ij} \qquad (2.9$$

b_j: the threshold of neural cells in the first hidden layer   .

q : the number of inputs

F_j (.):The activation function of neural cells, the first hidden layer

Let m_2 be the number of neural cells in the second hidden layer

The output of this layer is described as follows: f_k and It can be written as follows equation[50] :

$$\sum^{m1} b_j + f_j w_{jk} \tag{2.1}$$

Where   :

b_k: the threshold of neural cells of the hidden layer second.

We can calculate the production of the final layer according to the following equation[51].

$$\sum^{m2} b_l + f_l . w_{l.l} \tag{2.1}$$

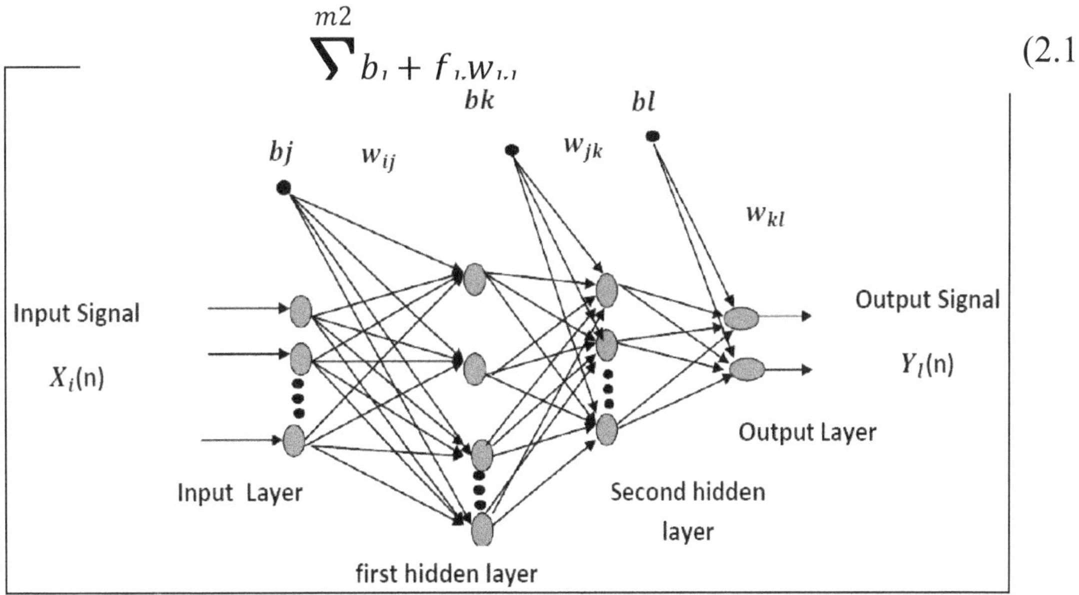

Figure(2.6): MLP Architecture

Where b_l is the neuron threshold for the final g layer m_3 is the number of neural in the production layer and can express the output of MLP

$$Y_l\,(n) = F_n\left[\sum_k^{m2} F_k w_{kl}\ \left(\sum_j^{m1} F_j w_{jk}\ \left\{\sum_i^{N} b_j + x_{i(n)} w_{ij}\right\} + bk\right) + bl\right] \tag{2.}$$

2.4 Morphology Operator

The word Morphology, as defined, is a branch of Biological Sciences that deals with the shape and structure of animals and plants. In the image processing field, Mathematical Morphology is used to define and extract useful information from the image based on the properties of the composition or shape within that image. Morphology can be applied to all

types of images (RGB, grey, binary). The process depends on the composition of the group theory[52,53]. The target from ways synthetics is the mathematical definition of the structure of the object based on a set of relations between the different parts of that object. Thus, the theory of the mathematical structure sees the image through the perspective of its geometrical structure, which distinguishes it from the rest of the theories of image processing. In mathematical methods, a number of operations are known to modify the shape of an image that has the name (x) by another form symbolized by a specific symbol such as the symbol (B), which is known as the structure element and from these structural processes Dilation, Erosion, Opening, Closing[54].

2.4.1 Structural Element of Morphology

It is a small group used to investigate the image .It can be used to explore the geometric structure of the objects within the digital image. The structural element is either a flat level used to handle gray and binary images or an uneven (not flat) level used to process RGB images. Basic structural processes require the determination of the origin of the structural element.

The shape and size of the structural element must match the geometric characteristics of the objects in the image to be treated within the image. For example, the structure that forms a suitable line for extracting linear objects from the image   Shows(2.7) some common forms of the structural element[55].

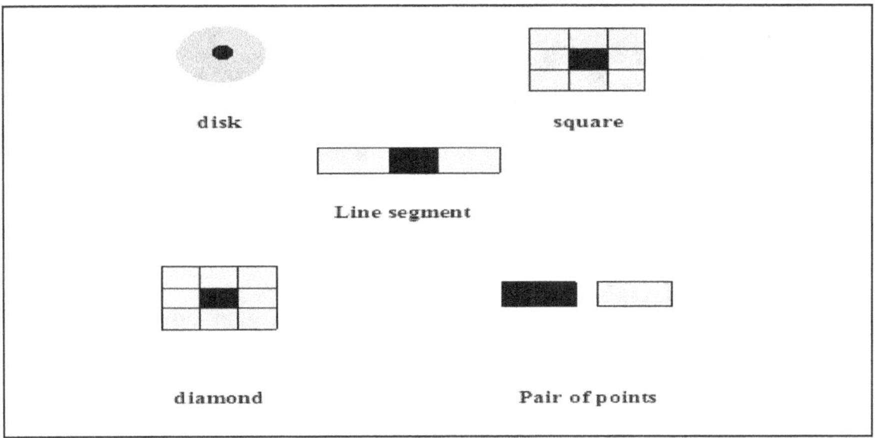

Figure (2.7) Common forms of a structural element

2.4.1.1 Erosion Detection

It's the main way of the Erosion morphology is may be applied in many techniques and can also be combined with dilation to create many types (opening, closing) is usually used in the binary images (black and white). The erosion of image g is given by the structure of element s by $g \ominus r$. The structure element r is placed with its origin in (x, y) and the new pixel value is determined using the rule in equation (2.13). Figure(2.8) represents a corrosion process[56,57].

$$t(x,y) \begin{cases} I & \text{if } r \text{ fits } g \\ 0 & \text{otherwise} \end{cases} \qquad (2.$$

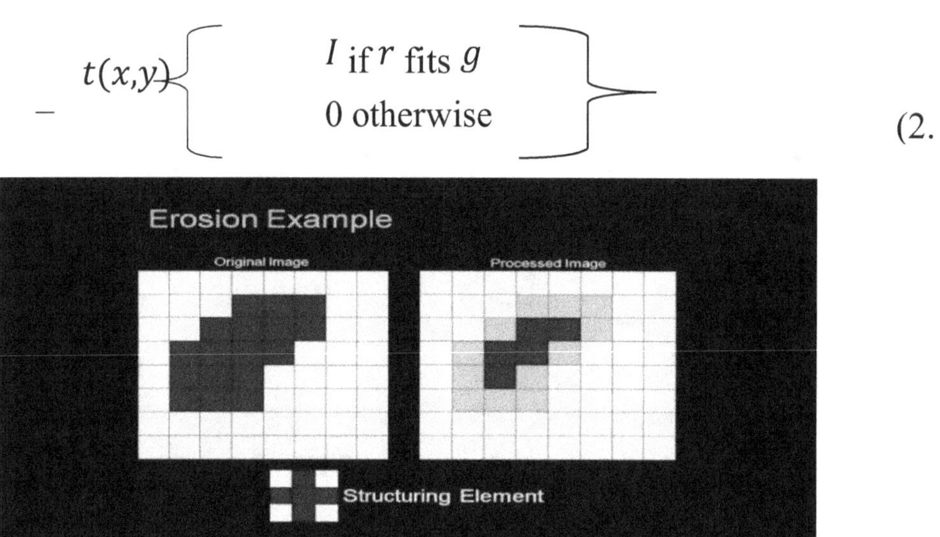

Figure (2.8): The impact of erosion

2.4.1.2 Dilation Detection

It's one of the ways of Dilation morphology. It can be applied in several techniques in addition to the possibility Merge with erosion to the creation of several types (opening, closing) and commonly used in the binary system images (black and white) and the expansion of pixels interested in pixels in the neighbourhood, the expansion of white pixels. The width of the image g is given by the element of structure r by($g \oplus r$). The structure element s is placed with its origin at (x, y) and the new pixel value is specified using the rule in equation (2.14). Figure (2.9) dilation operation [56].

$$(2.14)$$

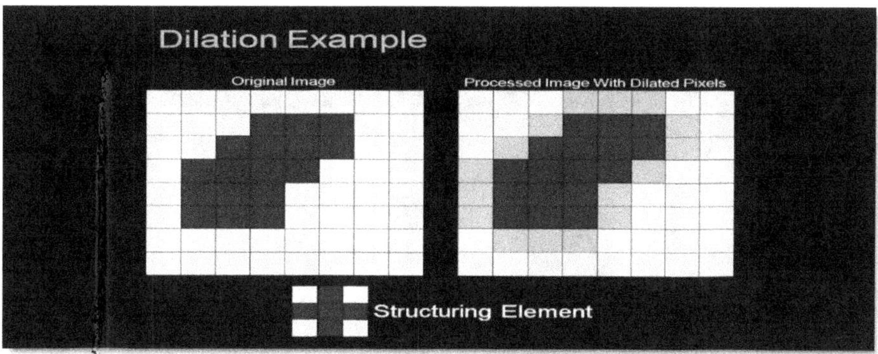

Figure(2.9): The impact of dilation

2.4.1.3 Compound Operations

The most exciting morphological operations can be obtained by evaluating both of erosions and dilations. The important and very used of these operations are   opening and closing [58].

A. Opening

The opening of image g by structuring element r denoted($g \circ r$) is nothing but an erosion followed by a dilation.Figure (2.10) represents the opening morphology

$$g \circ r = (g \ominus r) \oplus r \qquad (2.1$$

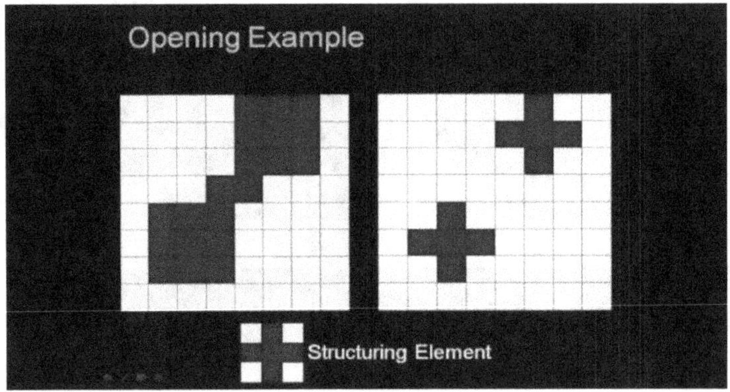

Figure (2.10): The effect of open morphology .

B. Closing

The closing of image g by means of structuring element r indicate $g \cdot r$ is simply a dilation followed pursued by an erosion as shown in equation (2.16). Figure (2.11) represents the closing morphology [58].

$$g \cdot r = (g \oplus r) \ominus r \qquad (2.1$$

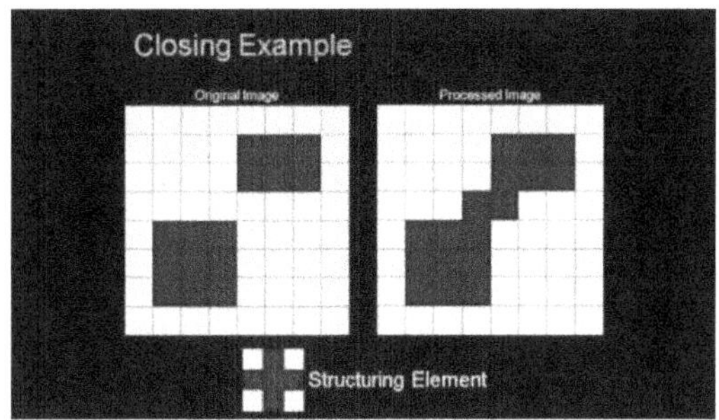

2.5 Ge

Figure (2.11): The impact of close morphology .

Geometric features are the features of the objects that have been created by a group of geometric elements like points, lines, curves or surfaces. In our proposed Algorithm then are a set of measurements

(Euclidean distance, Slope, Area, Perimeter, Centroid and Extrema Points, Angle and Rotation) to extract the features of the hand gesture as better than the others; the mathematical description of these measurements is given below:

2.5. 1 Euclidean distance

The Euclidean distance is the space between two points in Euclidean space. The two points V and P in two-dimensional Euclidean spaces [59].

If $V = (v_1, v_2)$, $P = (p_1, p_2)$ are two points, then the Euclidean Distance between V and P is given by:

$$EU(V,P) = \sqrt{(v_1 - p_1)^2 + (v_2 - p_2)^2} \qquad (2.1$$

) and P =(v_n, ...,v_2, v_1 if the points have n dimensions, such as V=(

) then, eq. (2.17) can be generalized by defining the Euclidean p_n ,...,p_2,p_1

distance between V and P as

$$(2.1$$

$$EU(V,P) = \sqrt{(v_1 - p_1)^2 + (v_2 - p_2)^2 + ... + (v_n - p_n)^2}$$

2.5.2 The Slope

The straight line is   a set of points that which has a fixed slope between any two points. The slope of the straight line is usually determined

by the value of the ratio of vertical change to horizontal variation. The slope usually describes the slope of the two-point line. The parallel line of the x-axis is defined as the horizontal line, Zero. The parallel line of the y-axis is known as the vertical line, and its slope always has an undefined value. The

parallel two lines always have slope equal[60].This is described by the following equation (2.19).

$$Slope = \frac{yz - yo}{xz - xo} \qquad (2.$$

2.5.3 The Area

The area is the extension of shapes, and it is different from the perimeter. Where the linked inside the shape, there are many known formulas for simple forms such as triangles, rectangles, and circles. Using these formulas, any polygon area can be calculated by dividing the polygon into triangles or circles to obtain curved shapes with borders and then collected after the calculation of their areas and when the polygon is

irregular can   polygon area is calculated by   equation   Gauss trapezoidal and described as in the following equation (2.20) [61].

$$A = \frac{1}{2}\sum_{i=0}^{n-1}(x_i * y_{i+1}) - (x_{i+1} * y_i)$$

(2.2

n: number of points

x_i : X axis coordinates

y_i : y axis coordinates

2.5.4 The Perimeter

The perimeter is the length of the line that surrounds the two-dimensional shapes, such as the circle, square, rectangle or irregular shapes. The perimeter can be calculated as in equation (2.21) if the shape is equilateral while the equation (2.22) calculates the perimeter if the shape is ribbing inequilaterally[62].

$$Per = n * (x) \qquad (2.2$$

$$Per = \sum_{i=0}^{n-1} x_i \qquad (2.2$$

n: Number of ribs

x:length of the rib

2.5.5 Centroid and Extrema point

The centroid is a fixed point in the object where the lines pass through this point which represents the weight of the object. The centroid is different from each other in terms of form or acclimatization and thus

determine the status of a centroid related to this difference. The centroid can be calculated according to the following equation(2.23)[63].

$$x_o = \frac{\sum x_{oi} A_i}{\sum A_i}, \; y_o = \frac{\sum y_{oi} A_i}{\sum A_i} \qquad (2.2$$

Where:

x_o: the x- axis value when center point of shape

y_o: the y- axis value when center point of shape

x_{oi}: The distance at which the center of the shape be far from the junction point of the axes on axis (x)

y_{oi}: The distance at which the center of the shape be far from the junction point of the axes on axis (y)

A_i: area the shape.

While Extrema point is (8*2) matrix that limits the extrema points in the region. Each row of the matrix has the x- and y-coordinates of one of the points. The format of the vector is (right-top, right-bottom, left-top, left-bottom ,top-right, top-left, bottom-right and bottom-left). This maybe is supported only for 2-D input label matrices .

2.5.6 Angle

Is the distance or break between the two straight lines converging with each other, where the intersection of the two lines and their intersection are called the angle head (Vertex), and the two line the two components of the

angle they know two ribs of the angle, The angle consists of two beams going from the same starting point . The angle is calculated any between the two intersectional   lines According to the following equation(2.24)[60]

$$angle = tan^{-1}(t_1 - t_2)/(1 + t_1 * t_2)) \qquad (2.2$$

t_1 : The slope between (B) and (A).

t_2 : The slope between (B) and (C).

2.5.7. Rotation

The rotation converts a pixel value from an original image to a new position in the rotated image by rotating it at a clockwise angle around the original. The rotation can be performed using the following equation (2.25) [64]:

$$\left.\begin{array}{l} \hat{z} = z * cos(\theta) - w * sin(\theta) \\ \hat{w} = z * sin(\theta) - w * cos(\theta) \end{array}\right\} \qquad (2.25)$$

Where:

(z, w) and $(\hat{z},\hat{w})$: are pixel coordinates before and after rotation, respectively,

θ : is the counter clockwise angle of rotation.

2.5.8 Mean

The mean is the numerical median of the data group. The mean is calculated by adding all the values in the group, Then divided the sum for the number of values in the group.

$$Mean = \sum_{i=0}^{m}\sum_{j=0}^{n}\frac{K(i,j)}{M} \qquad (2.2$$

Where

$k(i,j)$: value of object pixels.

n: height of the image.

m: width of the image.

M: count of the pixel.

2.5.9 Median

To know the value of median is first make by, descending or ascending, and then determine the value of the middle, where this value represents the value of the medium, but if there are two values are located in the middle, is taken the arithmetic mean of them, and then the output is the median.

2.6 Measurement Similarity ways

There are many ways for similarity measurements depending on the features obtains from the Algorithms or systems ,in this thesis we used three ways of measurements (Euclidean distance, Modify of the standardized Euclidean distance and correlations), where the modify of the standardized Euclidean distance gives most better results as will discuss in chapter 4.

2.6.1 Modify of the standardized Euclidean distance

It is one of the power at the way for measuring, it can be used for finding the similarity two points of vector or matrix the formula of modify of the standards Euclidean distance is as following[65].

$$Dst = \sqrt{\sum_{i=1}^{n} \frac{(x_i - y_i)^2}{\sqrt{\frac{1}{(n-1)}\sum_{j=1}^{n}(x_j - \overline{x})^2 + (y_j - \overline{x})^2}}} \qquad (2.2$$

Where :

x_i:is the ith valuse of first vector value.

y_i:is the ith valuse of second vector value.

n: is the number of elements in vector.

$\overline{x}$:is the mean value of first and second vector.

2.6.2 Correlation Coefficient [66]

The correlation's way is mostly used in objects analysis and image processing. We can use this way by comparing two vectors of image features of data features. As described in the following formula:

$$R1 = \frac{\sum\limits_{i}(x_i - x_m)(y_i - y_m)}{\sqrt{\sum\limits_{i}(x_i - x_m)^2}\ \sqrt{\sum\limits_{i}(y_i - y_m)^2}}$$

Where x_i is the intensity of the ith value in $vector$ 1, y_i is the intensity of the ith value in $vector$ 2, x_m is the mean intensity of $vector$ 1, and I is the mean intensity of $vector$ 2 .

2.6. 3 Euclidean distance

The Euclidean distance is one of the most important measuring ways used to draw the similarity between two vectors (testing vector with dataset vector). The formula of the Euclidean distance is shown in equation (2.17,2.18).

CHAPTER THREE
THE PROPOSED ALGORITHM

Chapter Three

The Proposed Algorithm

3.1 Introduction

This chapter provides an overview of the proposed Algorithm for gesture differentiation. As we mention that the main idea of our proposed Algorithm is to build a system for Hand Gesture Recognition for dumb and blind Social Communication by providing better and more reliable results. The final result will be a voice to make the blind hear the (letters, numbers, and words) from the dumb.

3.2   Proposed Algorithm

The proposed Algorithm contains two parts; the first part is the training by using   814 images while the second part is the testing by using 57 images as shown in Figure (3.1). The training part contains three phases, the first phase has two steps; first step is by record the video and the second is converted it into frames (images). The second phase contains four steps; image acquisition, pre-processing, segmentation, and features extraction. The third phase is classification phase where the image will be arrange by clusters or classes into 57 types(28 letters, 11numbers, 18 words) by using one of Algorithm (K-means, K medoid, ANN and C4.5) as shown in Figure(3.1.(a)).

The testing part contains four phases; the first phase has two steps; record the video and then convert it into frames (images). The second phase consists of four steps; image acquisition, pre-processing, segmentation, and features extraction. The third phase is classification phase where the image will be in cluster or class into 57 types(28 letters, 11numbers, 18 words) by comparing the feature vector with the 814 vectors stored in training part then the result will convert the class type or cluster type into corresponding voice (letters, numbers, and words) as shown in Figure (3.1.(b)).

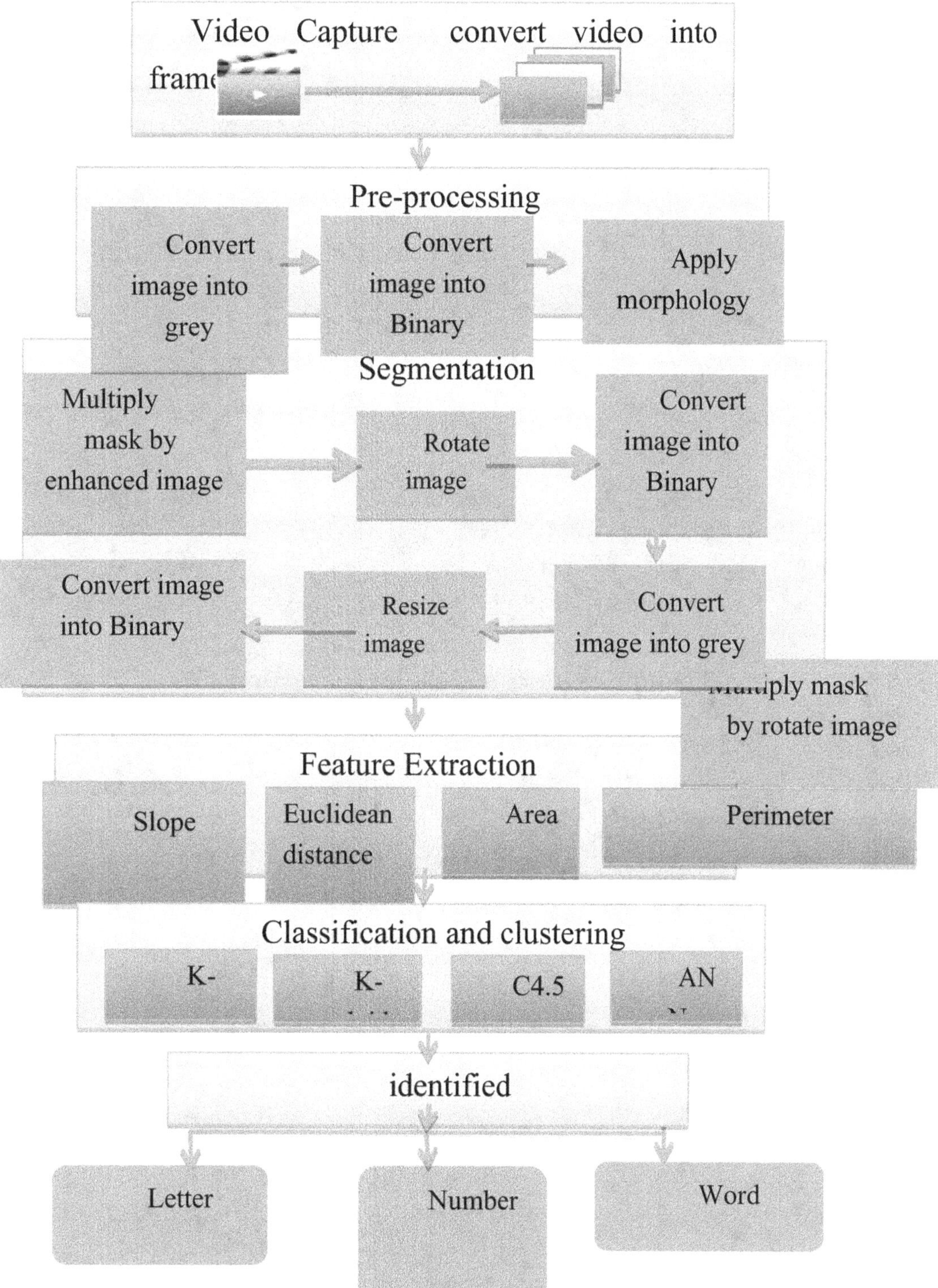

Figure(3.1.(a)):the proposed algorithm(training

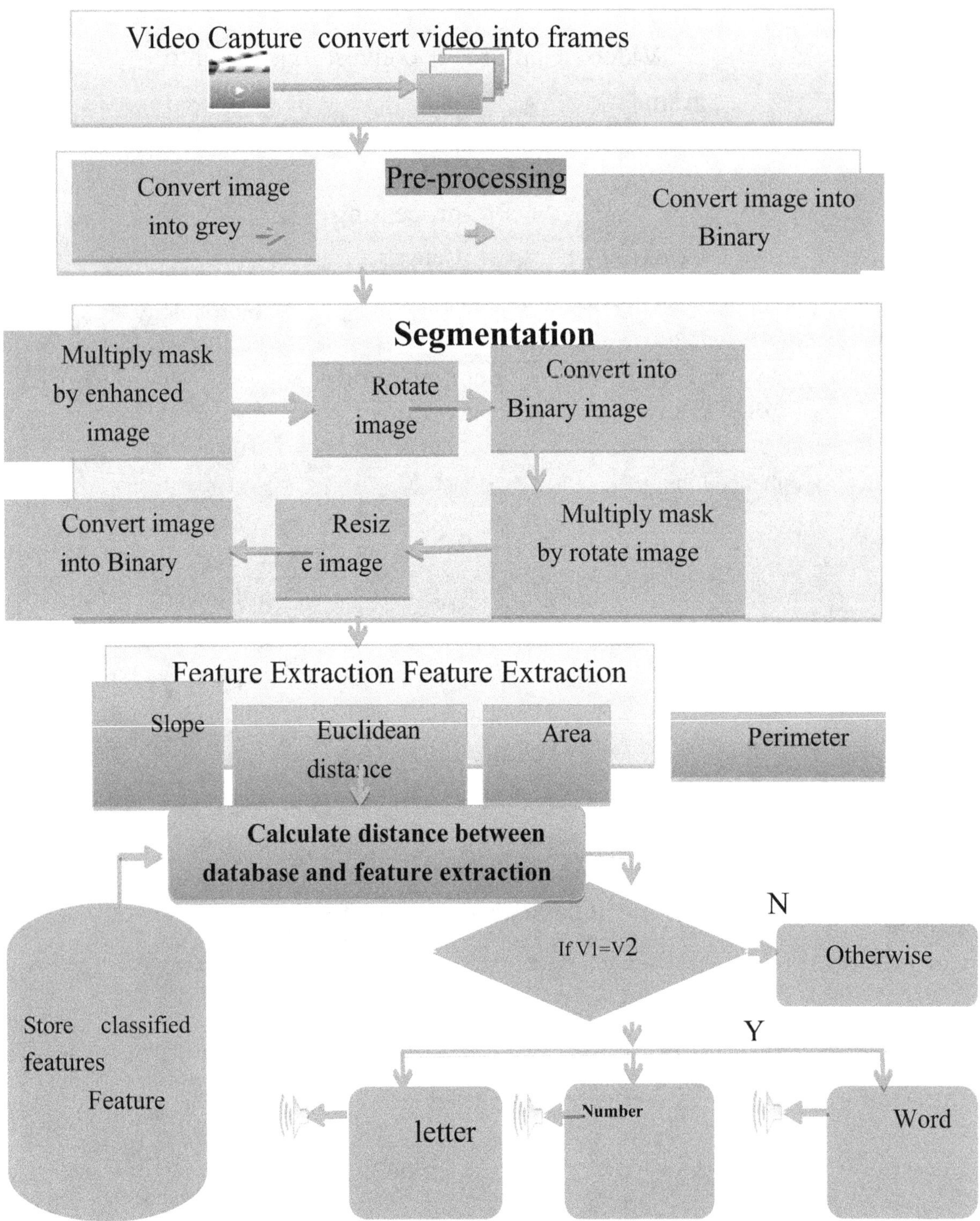

Figure(3.1.(b)): the proposed Algorithm(testing stage)

3.2.1.Digital video

Digital video is an electronic representation of the transmission of digital images in the form of encoding digital data. The video structure components are represented by the following:

a. Original Video (Image and Audio)

b. Shots

c. Scenes

d. Frames

e. Audio Track

3.2.1.1. Read video and convert it into frames

A video represents the gesture (signal) of the dumb by using an external camera and convert the video into frames we create more than ten videos from different people by using different cameras. This step can be implemented in the Algorithm (3.1)

<table>
<tr><td>

Algorithm (3.1) Read video and convert into frames

Input : video

Output : frames (Image Acquisition (Sign))

</td></tr>
<tr><td>

Begin

Step 1 : Read video

Step2: Video into frames

Step3:Read frames with period (1- 40)f/s

Step4:View frames

Step5:Save frames

End

</td></tr>
</table>

3.2.2 Pre-processing

In this step, we need to make all images have the same environments so we need the following:

3.2.2.1 Image Conversion

In this step, the color image will be converted from RGB format into the grey image by using the equation (3.1)[67]. The RGB image is composed of 24 bits (3* 8-bit) color (red, green, blue), while the grey image is made up of 8-bit value is (0 to 255). Taking the value of the color red, green, blue . And then convert the resulted image into a double image. When the frame is not RGB any gray frame convert frame into double image

.

$$grey\ image = (0.3R + 0.59G + 0.11B) \qquad (3.1)$$

3.2.2.2 Threshold image

The division of the image into homogeneous areas is a continuous and important research in the computer vision field. The threshold for the image is the best technique in frame segmentation, which is defined as a clustering of the image into homogeneous areas. The image representation is analytical and plays a very important role in several tasks in method technique identifying patterns and vision. The definition of the threshold is clearer. It is the technique of dividing the color or gray image based on the color value or the gray level, which transforms the image into a binary image by converting each element to the binary value of 0 or 1 depending on the probability of existence. Outside or within a specific range.

3.2.2.3 Dilation Morphology

Identical to convolution properties, one needs to suppose the image domains that are large sufficient then operations don't "fall " the edges. Dilation with 2*2 or 3*3…etc. structuring elements reduces the image by stripping boundaries of pixels from both the in and out boundaries of the image. The gaps & Holes between different areas become larger, and small specifies are eliminated. Algorithm (3.2) gives the steps of this operation

Algorithm (3.2): Dilation Operation

Input : binary image

Output : Dilation image

      Begin

Step 1: structuring element(3*3) =[1,1,1,1,1,1,1,1,1]

Step 2 : For each background pixel in binary image

        Maximum Value ← 0
        For each (3x3) pixel neighbours by structuring element
            Get pixel from binary image
            If pixel > Maximum Value then
                Maximum Value ← pixel
            End If
        End For
        Dilation image (pixel)← Maximum Value
      End For

End

3.2.2.4 Noise Removing with Close Morphology

The image that is extracted from dilation morphology at some time contains noise. This pixel can't be digit and therefore it is necessary to remove this noise pixel. The expression of closing as Dilation followed by Erosion is illustrated in Algorithm (3.3).

Algorithm (3.3): Close Morphology Operation

Input : Dilation image

Output : Close Morphology image

Begin

Step 1: structuring element(3*3) =[1,1,1,1,1,1,1,1,1]

Step 2 : For each background pixel in   Dilation image

Minimum Value ← 1
For each (3x3) pixel neighbours by structuring element
Get pixel from Dilation image
If pixel < Minimum Value then
Minimum Value ← pixel

End If
End For
Close Morphology image (pixel)← Minimum Value
End For
End

3.2.3 Segmentation

We need to segment the hand only and remove the background ,so the following steps are explain the segmentation:

3.2.3.1 Multiply mask by enhanced image

To segment an image of the resulted image (contain the only hand) and that by striking it with a mask of the hand size, then take the resulted image from the closing morphology process to extract a mask then multiply the mask by image resulted from the image conversion. Algorithm (3.4) explain the steps of segmentation.

Algorithm (3.4): Multiply mask by enhanced image

Input : Close Morphology image, Enhanced image

Output :image contain hand only

Begin

Step1: Determine the first and last column of resulted image (close Morphology). which contains pixel values (1).

Step2 Determine the first and last row of resulted image (close Morphology). which contains pixel values (1).

Step3: Create a mask with the same number of columns and rows that were determined in step (1) and step (2).

Step4: multiply the enhanced image with the mask specified in the step 3 so that the resulted image contain hand image only .

End

3.2.3.2 Orientation

Angle measurement ($+90°$ to $-90°$) between the axis (X) and the main axis of the ellipse. Algorithm (3.5) gives the steps of this operation

---

Algorithm (3.5):Orientation

Input : Close Morphology image

Output :Angle(Θ)

Begin

Point1=A , Point2=B , Point3=C .

Step 1: Calculate the slope between the coordinates of points (A) and (B) according to equation (2.19) .

Step 2: Calculate the slope between the coordinates of points (C) and (B) according to equation (2.19) .

Step 3: Calculate the angle according to equation (2.24) .

End

3.2.3.3 Rotation

Rotate converts the pixel value in the resulting image from the algorithm(3.4). to a new position in the rounded image at a clockwise angle around the point of origin. Algorithm (3.6) gives the steps for this operation

Algorithm (3.6):Rotation

Input : image hand

Output : rotation image

Begin

Step1: If angle is > 45

Rotate the image by equation (2.25) when it is   angle =sin(Θ)*(90-$|\Theta|$)

Else

Rotate the image by equation (2.25) when it is angle=sin(Θ)*($|\Theta|$)

End if

step2; rotation image $\leftarrow$ image hand

End

3.2.3.4 Threshold image

Convert the resulting image from the rotation step to a binary image .

3.2.3.5 Multiply mask by rotation image

To segment an image of the resulted image (contain the only hand) is by striking it with a mask of the hand size. Then take the resulted image from the binary image process to extract a mask .Then multiply the mask by image resulted from the Algorithm (3.6) . Algorithm (3.7) explains the steps of segmentation.

Algorithm (3.7): Multiply mask by rotation image

Input : Binary image, Rotation image

Output :image contain hand only

Begin

Step1: Determine the first and last column of resulted image (binary image). which contains pixel values (1).

Step2 Determine the first and last   row of resulted image (binary image). which contains pixel values (1).

Step3: Create a mask with the same number of columns and rows that were determined in step (1) and step (2).

Step4: multiply the rotation image with the mask specified in the step 3 so that the resulted image contain hand image only .

End

3.2.3.6 Image resize

In this step, the image resize the resulted image to make all images have the same size (any*100 pixels).

3.2.3.7 Threshold image

Convert the resulting image from the image resize step to a binary image .

3.2.4 Feature Extraction

In the proposed Algorithm, there are 18-geometrics features for each frame (image) these 18 features divided into three sets; the first set is

consist of (8-features) from calculate the distance between the 8 points with the center of hand and divide the distance length the hand, the second set also include (8-features) from calculate the slope of these 8 points in the first set and calculate the (inverse tan) slope, the third set consist from(2-features) the first one calculates the area of hand (and divide result on 10000) and second feature calculates the Perimeter   of   hand (and divide result on 500). Algorithm (3.8) gives the steps for this operation.

<table>
<tr><td>

Algorithm (3.8): Feature Extraction

Input : Binary Image

Output : Features Extraction

</td></tr>
<tr><td>

Begin
Step1: Extract 8 points of hand as shown in   Figure (3.2)
Step2: Calculate the area of hand as according to equation(2.20) and
      divided the result on 10000.
Step3: Calculate center point of hand as according to equation(2.23)
Step4: Calculating the 8-features include the distance of 8 points by using
      the Euclidean distance from the center of hand to the 8- points
      according to equation (2.18) and calculate the length of the hand and
      divide the distance by the length of the hand.
Step5: The second 8-features include the slop from the center of hand to the
      8-points as according to equation(2.19) then calculate (tan^{-1}) of
      the slope.
Step6: Calculate   Perimeter of hand   as according to equation(2.22) and
      divide the result by 500.
step7:Feature extraction ⬅   matrix [$distance$, slope , Area , perimeter].

</td></tr>
</table>

End

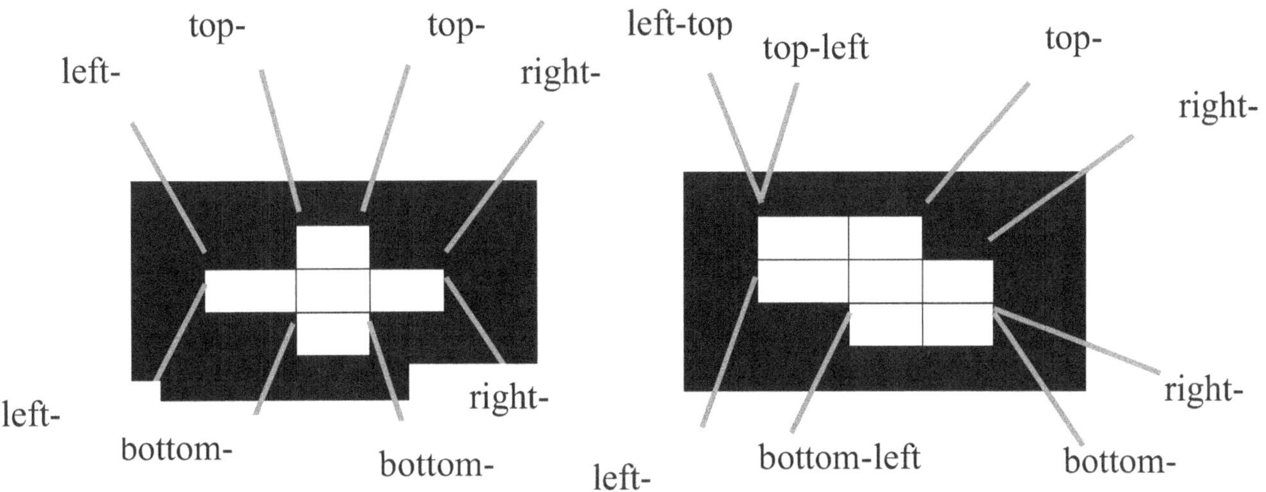

Figure(3.2) Extract 8 points of hand

3.2.5 Classification and clustering Algorithms

There are many Algorithms for clustering and classification , we found that the best four Algorithms as following:

3.2.5.1. C4.5 Algorithm

At this stage, the results of the previous stage are received, which are a value of 18, divided into four groups. Group one (distance) consisting of eight values, group two (slope) consisting of eight values, group three (area) consisting of one value and group four (perimeter) consisting of one value. Then, it is taken to extract valuable information Gain by Entropy. After that, a guess feature is done for each number and put it into an 18 - fields table. Algorithm (3.9) represent the C4.5 steps[68]:

Algorithm (3.9): C4.5 Algorithm

Input : Dataset Ds , Features Fs.

Output : Decision tree Tree.

<hr>

3.2.5.2. K-means Algorithm

After the feature extraction phase, the Algorithm k-means divides the input data into groups, in which each element is included in the section with the nearest central point (center), where the focal point represents the basis on which the data is divided and categorized.   The number of centers is (57) defined as the sum of letters (28) letters and numbers of (0-10) and (18) different words. The Algorithm (3.10) explains the steps of this process.

<table>
<tr><td>

Algorithm (3.10): K-means Algorithm

Input: Feature Extraction

Output: Group(Number or Letter or Word)

</td></tr>
<tr><td>

Begin

   Step1: Choose an initial mean array of the centroid for the first step, then calculate a new mean array of the centroid for other points in the next steps.

   Step2: Calculate the square of Euclidean distance betwee data object and cluster center as according to equation(2.18)

   Step3: Collect the data with the nearest center .

   Step4: Repeat steps 1 to 3 until stability (there are no objects moving within clusters), or even repetition a certain number of times.
   End

</td></tr>
</table>

3.2.5.3 K-medoid algorithm

After the feature extraction phase, the algorithm (k-medoid) divides the input data to aggregation blocks of the data entered into it into groups, thus reducing the distances between the data and the cluster centers. The number of medoids (57) is defined as the sum of letters (28) letters and numbers of (0-10) and (18) different words. The Algorithm (3.11) gives the steps for this process.

Algorithm(3.11):K-medoid Algorithm

Input :Feature Extraction

Output : A group of K cluster of(Number or letter or word)

Begin

A group of K cluster that decrease the aggregate of differences of every objects to their closest medoids .As shows in equation (3.2) [36].

$$Y = \sum_{i-1}^{k}\sum |z - m_i|$$
(3

Y: Sum of absolute error for every elements in the data collection.

z: The data point in the space representing a data item

m_i: is the medoid of cluster C_i

Step1: Choose array median initial medoid.

Step2: Set every residual data elements to a cluster with the closest medoid.

Step3: At random choose the non-medoid data component and calculate the total cost to swap the medoid data element for

---

the presently choose non-medoid data element .

Step4: If it is the total cost of the swap is minimal than zero, do the exchange process to create a novel group of k-midoids.

Step5: Reiterate steps 2, 3 and 4 untill the medoids stabilize their locations.

End.

3.2.5.4 Artificial neural network

After the feature extraction phase, the neural network Algorithm trains the features extracted in a neural network consisting of 18 inputs and 6 hidden layers to give one output. The Algorithm (3.12) gives the steps for this process.

Algorithm(3.12): ANN

Input: Feature Extraction

Output: Number or letter or word

Begin

Step1: input and target for ANN (18-input).

Step2: Use 6 hidden layer.

Step3: Training the ANN to set the weight.

Step4: Calculate the 6 output (numbers of (letter or number or word)).

End.

3.2.6 Text to Speech Converter

We convert text to Voice using the suggested Algorithm(3.13).

Algorithm(3:13): Text to speech Algorithm

Input: Editable text

Output: Speech

Begin

Step 1: prepare the record device (Microphone)

Step 2:

-Record Arabic letters from (أ- ي) .
-Record Arabic numbers from (0-10).
-Record Arabic word (18 words).

Step3:Play the voice (numbers, letters ,words) depending on to the

classification steps.

Step4: Save all record voices into voices dictionary that will be play

according to classification step.

End.

Chapter Four
IMPLEMENTATION AND TESTING THE ALGORITHM

Chapter four

Implementation and testing the Algorithm

4.1 Introduction

The experiments of the proposed Algorithm are executed by using four Algorithms for clustering and classifying the Arabic(Words, Letters, and Numbers) .These Algorithms were explained in Chapter Three. The results from these four Algorithms were different in accuracy ratio by using the same database, where these database collected from ten different videos which contain 814 frames (images) for both training and testing the results of the proposed Algorithm are described in next sections.

4.2 Data base

There is no database available (online) that can be used as a reference for other researchers, only some learning videos for learning words or numbers or letters. So we record 11 videos including (871) frames (images) as a database for our algorithm which divided into; ten videos for training stages with (814) images and one video with (57) images for testing.

4.3 Experimental Results   to read video and convert into frames

Figure (4.1) shows steps of capturing the video from the dumb and convert it into frames , where this video may be words or letters or numbers or all of them.

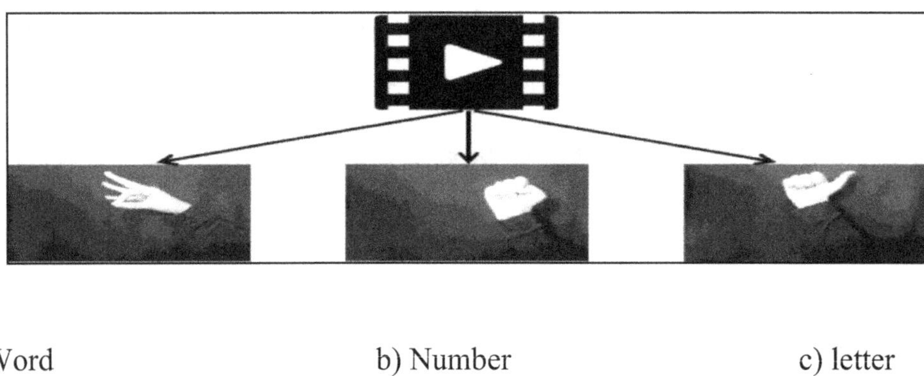

a) Word   b) Number   c) letter

Figure (4.1): Read video and convert it into frames

4.4. Pre-processing ,Segmentation and Feature Extraction

Figure (4.2) shows the pre-processing steps and segmentation of the proposed Algorithm for letter

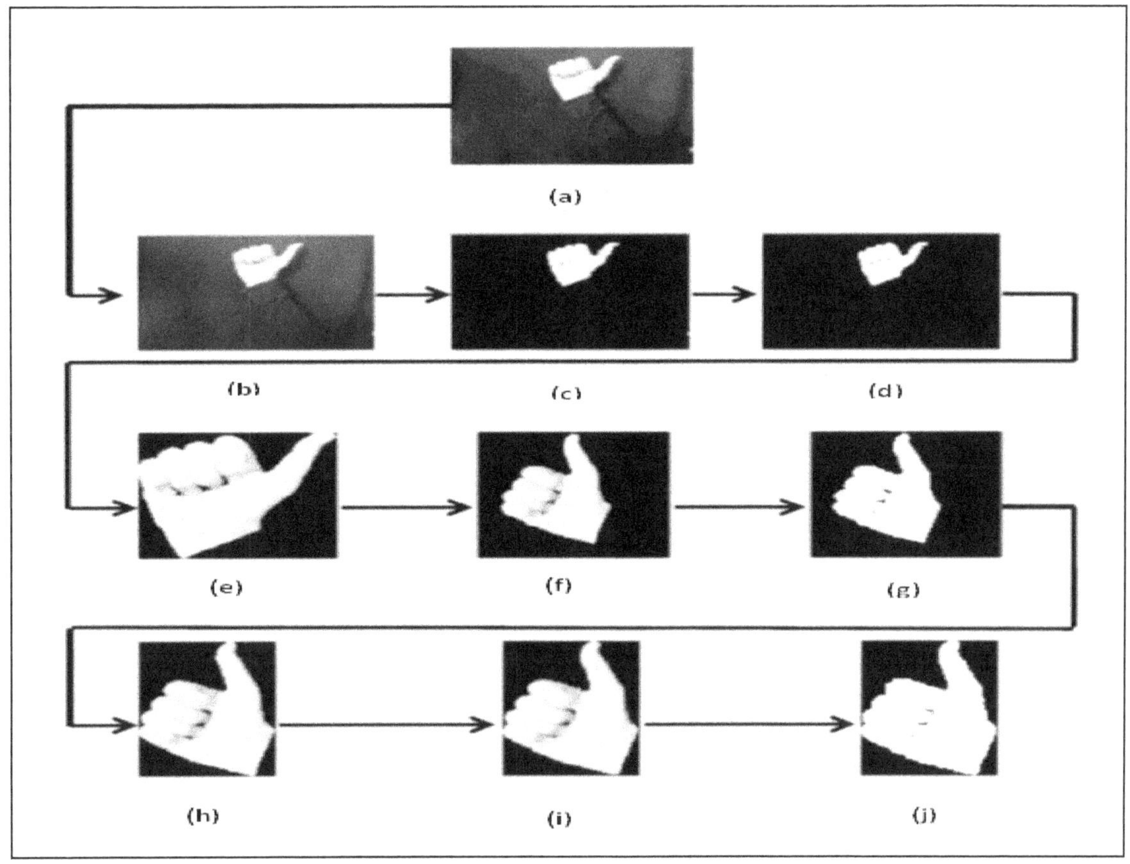

Figures (4.2): Sample of letter image after applying the pre-processing steps and segmentation. (a) Original image. (b) convert original image to grey level image. (c) convert the gray image into a binary image. (d) Apply morphological operation (e) segment hand (f) Rotate image (g) convert gray image into a binary image. (h) segment hand (i).Resize image. (j) convert the gray image into a binary image.

The resulted image will be located the centroid point and the Extrema   points   are determined as shown in Figure(4.3)

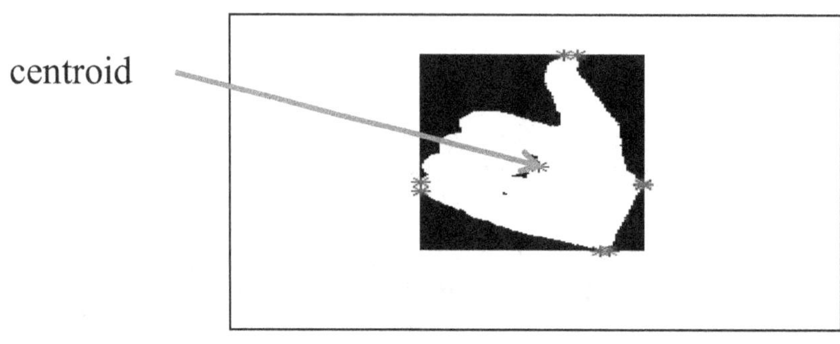

Figure (4.4) shows the pre-processing steps   and segmentation of the proposed Algorithm for numbers
(8 features for Distance) , (8 features for Slope) and (2 features for Area and Perimeter) as shown in Table (4.1) .

Table (4.1):Features vector of letter

Feature Geometry																	
Distance								Slope								Area	Perimeter
Dist1	Dist2	Dist3	Dist4	Dist5	Dist6	Dist7	Dist8	Sl1	Sl2	Sl3	Sl4	Sl5	Sl6	Sl7	Sl8		
0.2947	0.297	0.159	0.160	0.2366		0.189	0.182	-	-	1.313	1.293	0.440	0.401	-	-	0.828	0.891

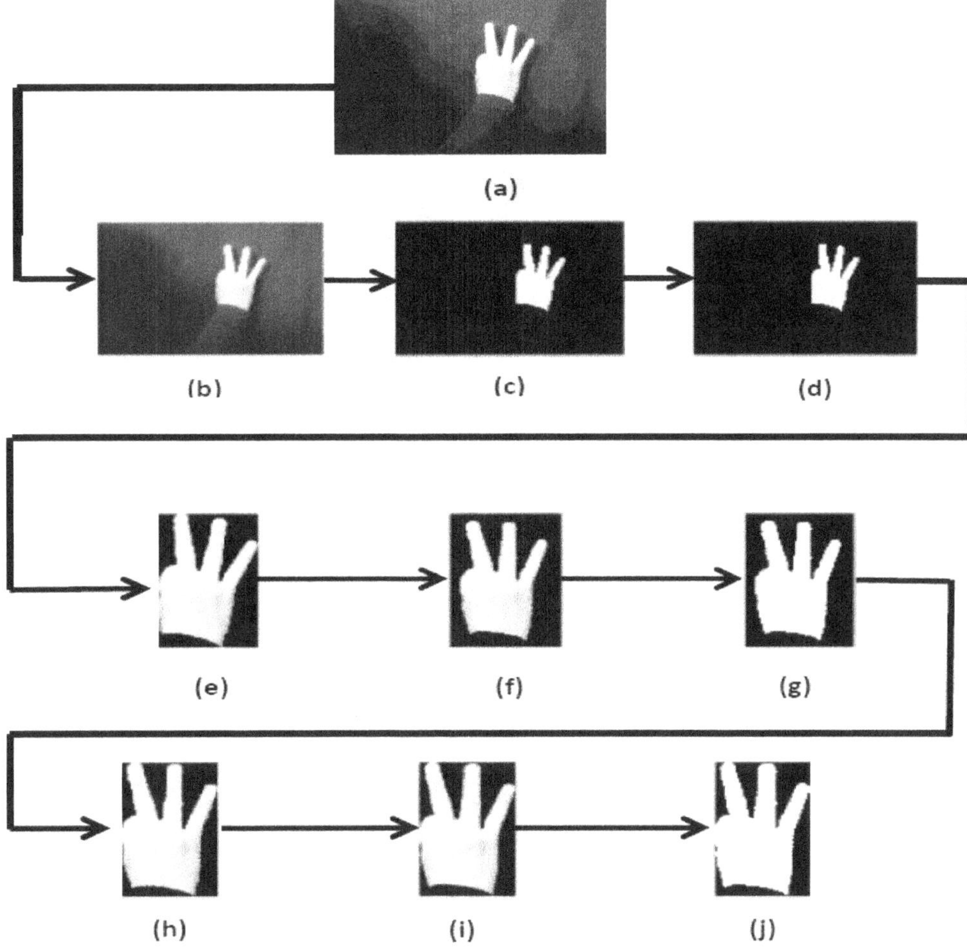

Figures (4.4): Sample of number image after applying the pre-processing steps and segmentation. ((a) Original image. (b) convert original image to grey level image. (c) convert the gray image into a binary image. (d) Apply morphological operation (e) segment hand (f) Rotate image (g) convert gray image into a binary image. (h) segment hand (i).Resize image. (j) convert the gray image into a binary image.

The resulted image will be located the centroid point and the Extrema points are determined as shown in Figure(4.5)

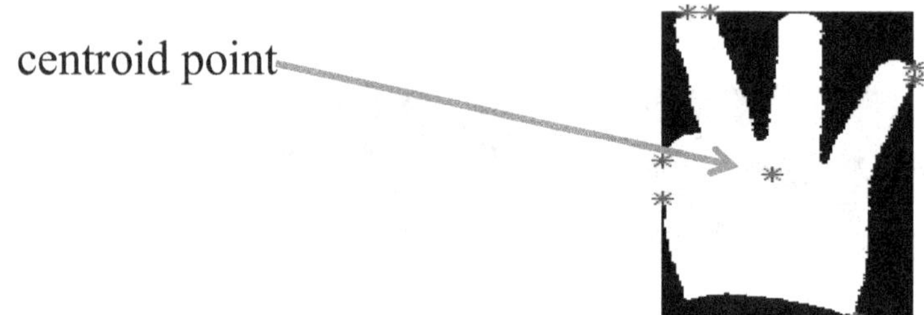

Figure (4.5) : the centroid point and extrema points

Table(4.2):Features vector of number

Then the features will extracted from the resulted image by calculating the 18 features (8 features for Distance) , (8 features for Slope) and (2 features for Area and Perimeter) as shown in Table (4.2) .

Feature Geometry																	
Distance								Slope								Area	Perimeter
Dist1	Dist2	Dist3	Dist4	Dist5	Dist6	Dist7	Dist8	Sl1	Sl2	Sl3	Sl4	Sl5	Sl6	Sl7	Sl8		
0.3361	0.3270	0.2793	0.2623	0.2980	0.2968	0.1546	0.1510	0.3488	0.2624	-0.7246	-0.7836	0.3727	0.3622	-1.2810	1.3765	1.0889	1.5166

Figure (4.6) shows the pre-processing steps   and segmentation of the proposed Algorithm for word

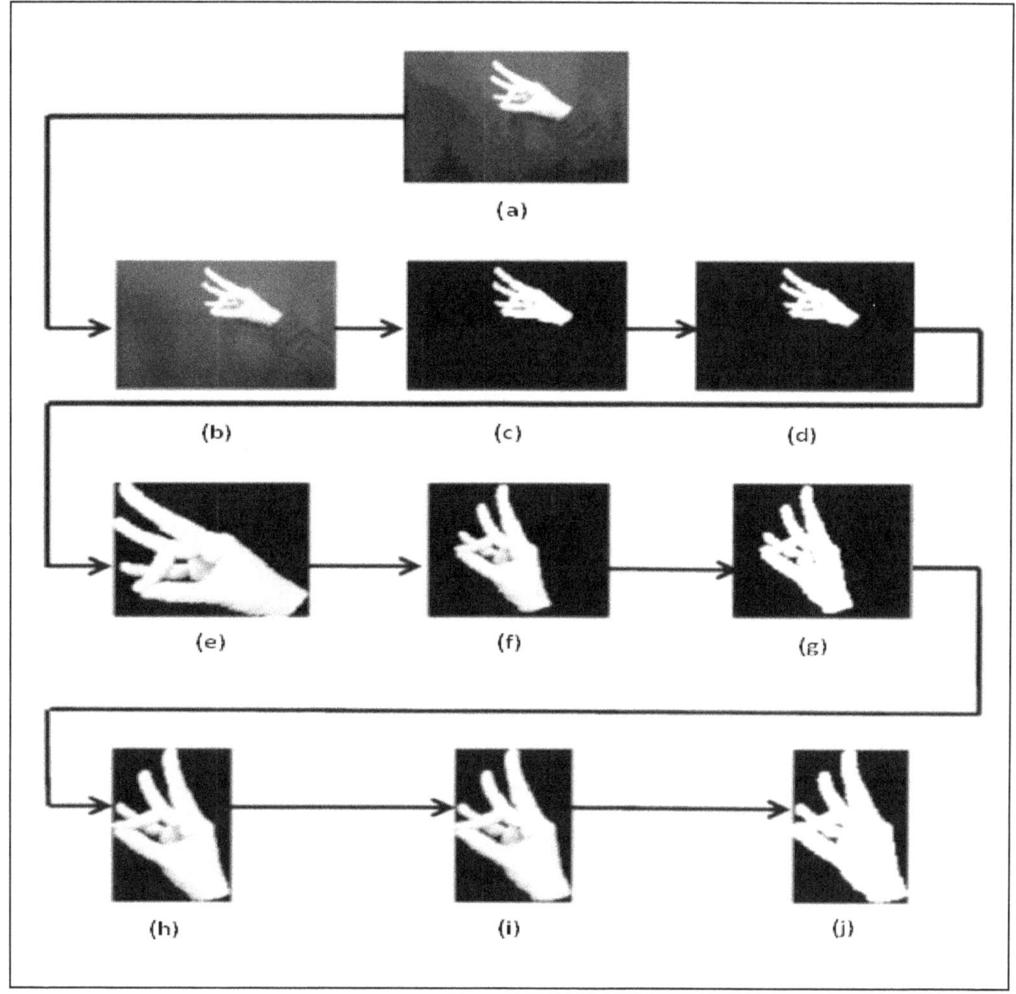

Figures (4.6): Sample of word image after applying the pre-processing steps and segmentation . (a) Original image. (b) convert original image to grey level image. (c) convert the gray image into a binary image. (d) Apply morphological operation (e) segment hand (f) Rotate image (g) convert gray image into a binary image. (h) segment hand (i).Resize image. (j) convert the gray image into a binary image.

The resulted image will be located the centroid point and the Extrema points are determined as shown in Figure(4.7)

centroid
point

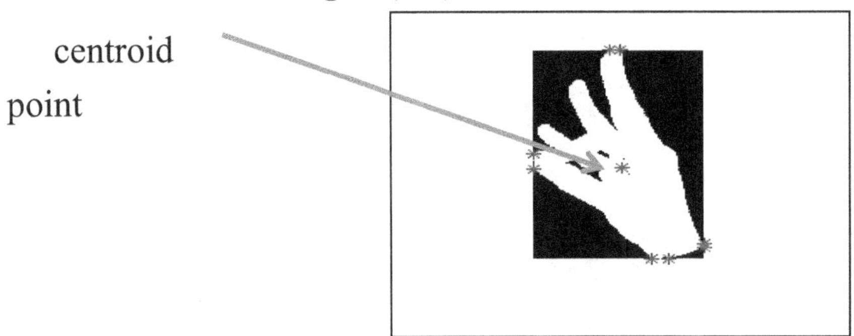

Figure (4.7):   the centroid point and extrema point

Then the features will extracted from the resulted image by calculating the 18 features (8 features for Distance) , (8 features for Slope) and (2 features for Area and Perimeter) as shown in Table (4.3) .

Table(4.3):Features vector of word

Feature Geometry																	
Distance								Slope								Area	Perimeter
Dist1	Dist2	Dist3	Dist4	Dist5	Dist6	Dist7	Dist8	Sl1	Sl2	Sl3	Sl4	Sl5	Sl6	Sl7	Sl8		
0.3136	0.3128	0.2628	0.2655	0.2569	0.2521	0.1760	0.1812	0.0725	-0.0020	0.6416	0.6341	0.3193	0.2565	-1.5676	1.3324	0.7795	1.1084

4.5. Calculate Mean and Median

1.   Calculate the Mean of features for the same letter or the same number or the same words from different images of the same (letter or number or word) as shown in Table (4.4)   where the mean of features calculated from 25 image for letter (أ), 17 image for number(3) and 15 images from word(انا بخير) .

Table (4.4): Features vector to sample of (letter or number or word)

Letter or number Or Word	Number of image	Feature Geometry																	
		Distance								Slope								Area	Perimeter
		Dist1	Dist2	Dist3	Dist4	Dist5	Dist6	Dist7	Dist8	Sl1	Sl2	Sl3	Sl4	Sl5	Sl6	Sl7	Sl8		
أ	25	0.32	0.32	0.15	0.15	0.23	0.23	0.19	0.18	-	-	0.91	0.97	0.45	0.40	-	-	0.83	1.11
3	17	0.311	0.302	0.255	0.247	0.273	0.270	0.160	0.149	0.272	0.083	-	0.0210	0.337	0.305	-	-	0.900	1.379
أنا بخير	15	0.2848201984766	0.2800988850579	0.2252943261582	0.2318671850505	0.2330555669152	0.2244522172933	0.1686207873870	0.1734031580116	0.2925694347661	0.2258617764167	0.8803379512937	0.8443058520956	0.5455634623551	0.4656238102982	-	1.0880246189357	0.5967733333333	1.0218666666666

2.   Calculate the Median of features for the same letter or the same number or the same words from different images of the same (letter or number or word) as shown in Table (4.5) where the mean of features calculated from 25 image for letter(أ) , 17 image for number (3) and 15 images from word (انا بخير) .

Table (4.5): Features vector to sample of (letter or number or word)

Letter or number Or Word	Number of image	Feature Geometry																	Area	Perimeter
		Distance								Slope									
		Dist1	Dist2	Dist3	Dist4	Dist5	Dist6	Dist7	Dist8	Sl1	Sl2	Sl3	Sl4	Sl5	Sl6	Sl7	Sl8		
أ	25	0.3284	0.3292	0.1591	0.1660	0.2326	0.2109	0.2053	0.1924	-0.0346	-0.0751	1.1948	1.1012	0.5489	0.3452	-1.1255	-1.2983	0.8397	1.2523
3	17	0.310	0.302	0.240	0.236	0.256	0.253	0.149	0.141	0.286	0.180	-	0.0250	-	0.286	0.248	-	0.781	1.317
أنا بخير	15	0.28	0.27	0.21	0.22	0.23	0.22	0.17	0.17	0.32	0.26	0.85	0.82	0.54	0.47	-	-	0.53	0.98

4.6 Results of the Four Algorithms

The result from Four Algorithms   (C4.5, K- mean, K-medoid   and ANN) in training stage where the training with database of 814 and the result had different classification rate, as shown in Table(4.6) and Figure (4.8) by using equation (4.1)[69].

$$Accuracy = ((TP + TN)/(TP + FP + FN + TN))100\%$$

Where TP Contains True Positives that properly classify positive states ,

FP is False Positives that improperly classify negative situations, TN is True Negative that properly classify negative states and FN is False Negative that is improperly classify positive states .

Table (4.6): the difference between Four Algorithms rate

Type	No image	C4.5	K-means	K-medoid	ANN
Letter	402	100%	96.1265 %	95.3269 %	93.0704 %
Number	162	100%	90.2357 %	87.5421 %	82.3793 %
Word	250	100%	95.2000 %	91.9111 %	91.2727 %
Mixed	814	99.8664 %	97.7930 %	97.3620 %	96.5386 %

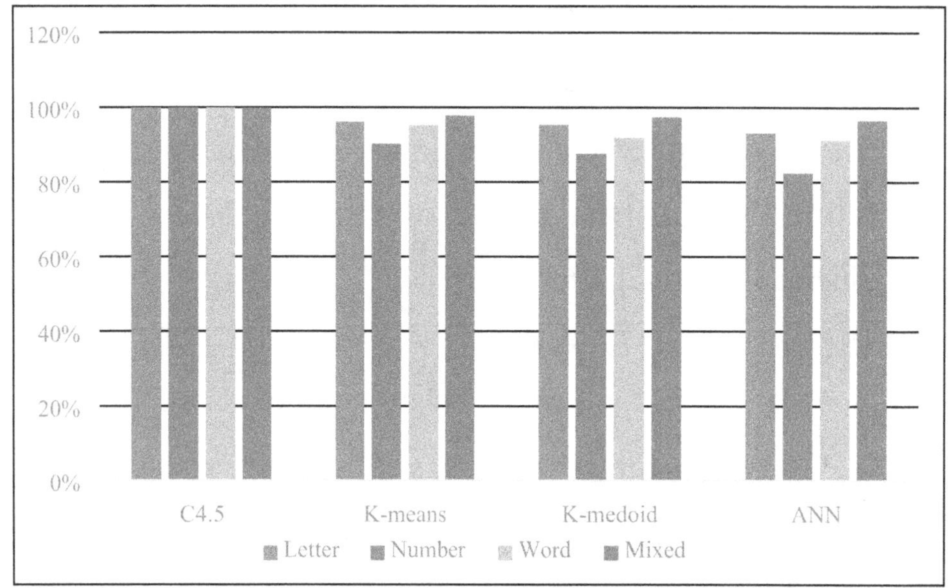

Figure (4.8): the difference between Four Algorithms rate

As shown in Table(4.6) and Figure (4.8) the C4.5 Algorithm is the best Algorithm in the classification and accuracy.

4.7. Testing results

The result from testing our Algorithm by using equation (2.27) to modify the standardized Euclidean distance (MSED) which compare the new features of image (letter, word or number) with the classified database images (classified in training by using C4.5) as shown in Table (4.7)and Figure(4.9)

Table (4.7): the accuracy rate of the MSED

Type	No image	No.data	Accuracy	Execution time
Letter	28	402	100%	3ms
Number	11	162	100%	3ms
Word	18	250	100%	3ms
Mixed	57	814	98.2456%	3ms

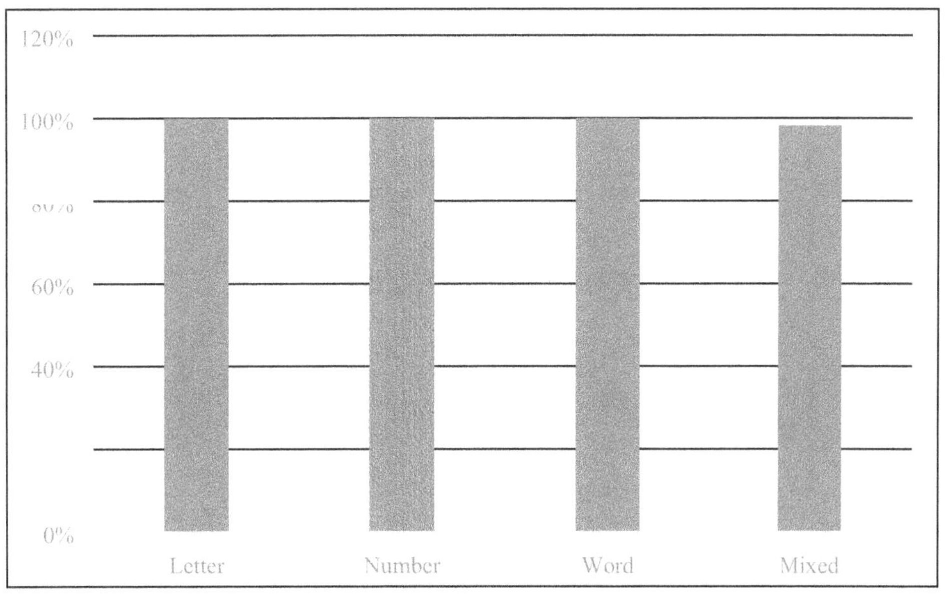

Figure (4.9): the accuracy rate using MSED

The result from testing our algorithm by using equation (2.28) of the correlation which compare the new features of image (letter, word or number) with the classified database images (classified in training by using C4.5) as shown in Table (4.8)and Figure(4.10)

Table (4.8): the accuracy rate using correlation

Type	No image	No.data	Accuracy	Execution time
Letter	28	402	100%	4ms
Number	11	162	100%	4ms
Word	18	250	94.4444%	4ms
Mixed	57	814	96.4912%	4ms

Figure (4.10): the accuracy rate using correlation

The result from testing our Algorithm by using equation (2.18) of the Euclidian Distance which compare the new features of image (letter, word or number) with the classified database images (classified in training by using C4.5) as shown in Table (4.9)and Figure(4.11)

Table (4.9): the accuracy rate using Euclidian Distance

Type	No image	No.data	Accuracy	Execution time
Letter	28	402	100%	2ms
Number	11	162	90.9091%	2ms
Word	18	250	94.4444%	2ms
Mixed	57	814	94.7368%	2ms

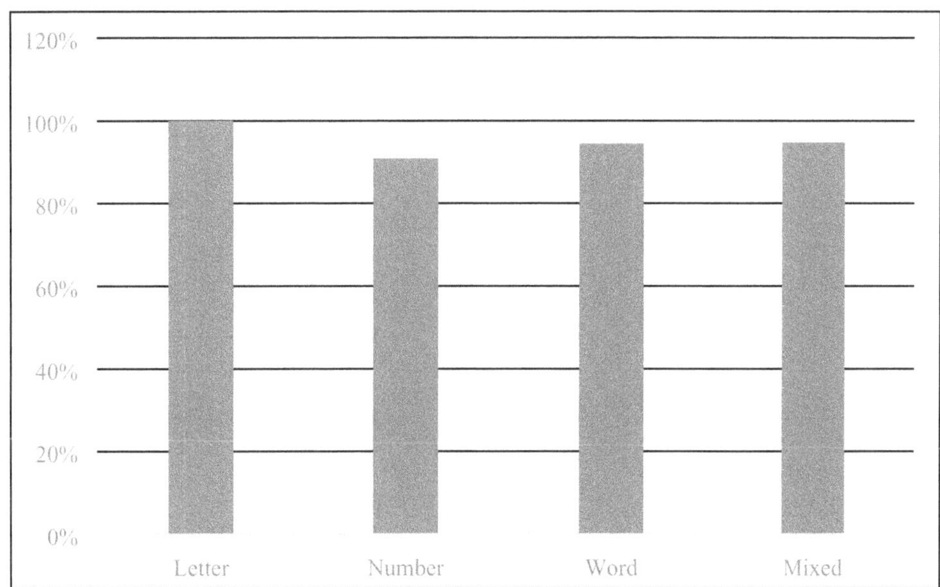

Figure (4.11): the accuracy rate using Euclidian Distance

The result shows that modify of the standardized Euclidean distance is the best accuracy from the correlation and Euclidian distance

4.8. Compare Algorithm with others

The comparison of others researchers with our Algorithm as shown in Table (4.10).There are many Algorithms or researchers for the gesture but no one uses mixed(letter, number, and word) at the same time. A most of them use one type (word or letter or number) and most of them didn't show the results from testing, only the use them Algorithm for training and it is easy to see the difference between our Algorithm with other researchers.

Table (4.10): The comparison of others researchers with our Algorithm

Reference	Size dictionary	No. of Features	Accuracy in Training %				Accuracy in Testing%			
			words	Letters	num	Mixed	word	letter	num	Mixed
[70]	10	6	90	-	-	-	-	-	-	-
	120	6	20	-	-	-	-	-	-	-
[71]	100	3	99.6	-	-	-	-	-	-	-
[72]	100	3	98.1	-	-	-	-	-	-	-

[73]	30	30	-	97.4	-	-	8 / 4.5	-	-
			-	98.4	-	-	9 / 3.4	-	-
[74]	30	30	-	95.1	-	-		-	-
			-	89.6	-	-		-	-
[75]	30	30	-	79.3	-	-	-	-	-
			-	84.5	-	-	-	-	-
[76]	23	2	87	-	-	-	-	-	-
[77]	23	2	About 95	-	-	-	-	-	-
[78]	50	4	98	-	-	-	-	-	-
[79]	300	4	95	-	-	-	-	-	-
[80]	28	1	-	80	-	-	-	-	-

[81]	40	5	70	-	-	-	-	-	-	-
[12]	30	3	-	95.5	-	-	-	-	-	-
[82]	50	3	98.1	-	-	-	-	-	-	-
[13]	20	8	82.2	-	-	-	-	-	-	-
[83]	28	1	-	97	-	-	-	-	-	-
[84]	30	3	-	91.3	-	-	-	-	-	-
		50	-	83.7	-	-	-	-	-	-
[85]	23	2	96	-	-	-	-	-	-	-
	80	2	75	-	-	-	-	-	-	-
[86]	28	1	-	90.5	-	-	-	-	-	-
[87]	30	8	-	97	-	-	-	-	-	-
Our algorithm	57	18	100	100	100	99.8	100	100	100	98.2

CHAPTER FIVE
CONCLUSIONS AND FUTURE WORKS

Chapter five

Conclusions and Future Work

5.1 Introduction

In this chapter, we relate the conclusions of the suggested algorithm from the experiments and results. We shall also provide suggestions for future work to help other researchers or developers.

5.2 Conclusions

From our experiments and results , we conclude the following points:

1. Morphology techniques are used to extract hand of hand image by using Dilation and the resulted image uses Close morphology to remove holes and breaks from processing an image conversion from the grayscale image to the binary image.

2. In our experiments, we found that the geometric features (distance, area, perimeter, and slope) are the best features compared with other features such as(shape, texture, color,…..etc).

3. In the testing stage, we found that to modification of the standardized Euclidean distance is the best metric for calculating the corresponding feature vector of the testing image, to know the type of which of 57 class (Letters, Words, Numbers) ,while others metrics such as (Euclidean distance, Correlation,….etc.) gave lower accuracy .

4. There are many clustering and classifying Algorithms used in our suggested Algorithm such as (K-means, K-medoid, C4.5, and ANN) .Yet, the experiments found that C4.5 Algorithm is the best one in classification   with the percentage of(99.8664) in training and (98.2456%) in testing.

5.3 Future work

During the period of work on this thesis, we found many ideas which represent the future work of this thesis. We can suggest the following points :

1. Designing a new Algorithm which may help social communication between the blind and the dumb, i.e., the opposite process of our current Algorithm starting from the sound of blind to the song for the dumb.

2. Using the same Algorithm (mixed words, letters, and numbers) with others languages (e.g., English, Indian, Chines, Persian…etc).

3. Building hardware devices to be used as translators or commentators between the dumb and the blind directly or indirectly.

4. Design Android software & hardware for the proposed system.

REFERENCES

References

[1]   Ch. V.N. Syam Babu, V.J.K. Kishor Sonti and Y. Varthamanan,"**Design and Simulation of Communication Aid for Disabled Using Threshold Based Segmentation**", I J C T A, 9(7), pp. 3275-3281,2016.

[2]   Kumud Tripathi ,Neha Baranwal and G. C. Nandi, **"Continuous Indian Sign Language Gesture Recognition and Sentence Formation"** , Procedia Computer Science ,54,pp. 523 – 531,2015.

[3]   Liu Yun, Zhang Lifeng and Zhang Shujun, **"A Hand Gesture Recognition Method Based on Multi-Feature Fusion and Template Matching"**, Procedia Engineering ,29,pp. 1678 – 1684,2012.

[4]   Hee-Deok Yang, **" Sign Language Recognition with the Kinect Sensor Based on Conditional Random Fields"**, Sensors, 15, pp. 135–147, 2015.

[5]   Pablo Barros, Nestor T. Maciel-Junior , BrunoJ.T. Fernandes , ByronL.D. Bezerra and Sergio M.M. Fernandes , **"A Dynamic Gesture Recognition and Prediction System Using The Convexity Approach"**, Computer Vision and Image Understanding, 155, pp. 139–149, 2017.

[6]محمد علي كامل , **" قاموس لغة الاشارة للأطفال الصم "** ,دار الطلائع ,القاهرة, 2004 .

[7]   Xu J, Gannon PJ, Emmorey K, Smith JF and Braun AR, **"Symbolic Gestures and Spoken Language are Processed by A common Neural System"**, Proc Natl Acad Sci U S A, 106,pp.20664–20669,2009.

[8] بيتركليتون, **" لغة الجسد مدلول حركات الجسد وكيفية التعامل معها "** ,دار الفاروق,2005.

[9] Allan and Barbara Pease,"**The Definitive Book of Body Language**", Pease International, Australia,2004.

[10] Klimis Symeonidis, **"Hand Gesture Recognition Using Neural Networks"**, the School of Electronic and Electrical Engineering , August 23, 2000.

[11] Jiuqiang Tang, **"Extracting Commands From Gestures: Gesture Spotting and Recognition for Real-time Music"**, Carnegie Mellon University,May,2013.

[12] Omar Al-Jarrah and Alaa Halawani ,**"Recognition of Gestures in Arabic Sign Language Using Neuro-Fuzzy Systems"**, Artificial Intelligence ,133 ,pp. 117–138,2001.

[13] Aliaa A. A.Youssif , Amal Elsayed Aboutabl and Heba Hamdy Ali, **"Arabic Sign Language (ArSL) Recognition System Using HMM"**, IJACSA, Vol. 2, No. 11,pp.45-51, 2011.

[14] S.S. Ge, Y. Yang and T.H. Lee ,**"Hand Gesture Recognition and Tracking Based on Distributed Locally Linear Embedding"**, Image and Vision Computing ,26 ,pp. 1607–1620,2008.

[15] Feng-Sheng Chen, Chih-Ming Fu and Chung-Lin Huang, **"Hand Gesture Recognition Using a Real-Time Tracking Method and Hidden Markov Models"**, Image and Vision Computing ,21 ,pp. 745–758,2003.

[16] Eldin Henry Shroffe D and   P.Manimegalai, **" Hand Gesture Recognition Based on EMG Signals Using ANN"**, International Journal of Computer Applicat, Issue. 3, Vol. 2 , pp.31-39,April ,2013.

[17] Zhi-hua Chen, Jung-Tae Kim, Jianning Liang, Jing Zhang and Yu-Bo Yuan, **"Real-Time Hand Gesture Recognition Using Finger Segmentation"**, the Scientific World Journal, Vol. 2014, Article ID 267872, pp.1-9,2014.

[18] Liu Yun, Zhang Lifeng and Zhang Shujun, **"A Hand Gesture Recognition Method Based on Multi-Feature Fusion and Template Matching"**, Procedia Engineering , 29, pp. 1678–1684, 2012.

[19] SUMAIRA KAUSAR, M. YOUNUS JAVED and SHALEEZA SOHAIL, **"Recognition of Gestures in Pakistani Sign Language using Fuzzy Classifier"**, 8th WSEAS International Conference on SIGNAL PROCESSING, COMPUTATIONAL GEOMETRY and ARTIFICIAL VISION (ISCGAV'08),pp.101-105, August 20-22, 2008.

[20] Mathavan Suresh Anand, Nagarajan Mohan Kumar and Angappan Kumaresan**, "An Efficient Framework for Indian Sign Language Recognition Using Wavelet Transform"**,Scientific Research publishing,7,pp. 1874-1883,2016.

[21] Himanshu Kumar, **"Gesture Recognition Using Hidden Markov Models Augmented with Active Difference Signatures"** , RIT Scholar Works,2014.

[22] Oi Mean Foong, Tan Jung Low, and Satrio Wibowo, **"Hand Gesture Recognition: Sign to Voice System (S2V)"** , International Journal of Electrical and Electronics Engineering, ISBN 3-4,pp.198-202,2009.

[23] Mahmoud Elmezain, Ayoub Al-Hamadi, and Bernd Michaelis, **"Hand Gesture Recognition Based on Combined Features Extraction"** , International Journal of Electrical and Computer Engineering, Vol.3, No.12, 2009.

[24] Shu-Fai Wong and Roberto Cipolla, **"Continuous Gesture Recognition Using A Sparse Bayesian Classifier"** ,Proceedings of the 19th International Conference on Pattern Recognition(ICPR'06),Aug20-24,2006.

[25] P. V. Waje, Pagar Priyanka Sampat, Gade Kanchan Dinesh, Kharjul Priyanka Sanjay and Hon Suchet Sudhakar, **"A Narrative Technology For Communication Among Blind, Deaf And Dumb People"**, International Journal of Informative & Futuristic,Vol.3,Issue .7,pp.2363-2369,March,2016.

[26]　　Deepti Sisodia, Lokesh Singh, Sheetal Sisodia and Khushboo saxena , **" Clustering Techniques :A Brief Survey of Different Clustering Algorithm"** , International Journal of Latest Trends in Engineering and Technology (IJLTET), Vol. 1 ,Issue .3,pp.82-87, September, 2012.

[27]　　Vladimir Estivill-Castro, **"Why So Many Clustering Algorithms – A Position Paper"** , ACM SIGKDD Explorations Newsletter, 4 (1),pp.65–75, 20 June ,2002.

[28] M. Emre Celebi , Hassan A. Kingravi and Patricio A. Vela, **"A Comparative Study of Efficient Initialization Methods for The K-means Clustering Algorithm"** , Expert Systems with Applications,40,pp.200-210,2013.

[29] Sadina Gagula-Palalic**, "Fuzzy Clustering Models and Algorithms for Pattern Recognition"** , Ph.D. International University of Sarajevo Mechatronics and System Engineering Graduate Program, Sarajevo, 2008.

[30] Maria Halkidi, Yannis Batistakis, Michalis Vazirgiannis , **"On Clustering Validation Techniques"** , Journal of Intelligent Information Systems, 17:2/3,pp. 107–145, 2001.

[31] T. Velmurugan,and T. Santhanam, **"A Survey of Partition Based Clustering Algorithms in Data Mining: An Experimental Approach"** , Anexperimental approach Information Technology Journal, Vol . 10,No .3 , pp478-484,2011.

[32] S. C. Johnson, **"Hierarchical Clustering Schemes"** ,*Psychometrika*, Vol. 32, no. 3, pp. 241–254, 1967.

[33] Mohammad Hasanzadeh-Mofrad and Alireza Rezvanian, **" Learning Automata Clustering"** ,Journal of computation science,2017.

[34] Jyoti Yadav and Monika Sharma, **"A Review of K-mean Algorithm"** , International Journal of Engineering Trends and Technology (IJETT) , Vol. 4, Issue. 7,pp.2972-2976, July ,2013.

[35] Preeti Arora, Dr. Deepali and Shipra Varshney, **"Analysis of K-Means and K-Medoids Algorithm For Big Data"** , Procedia Computer Science ,78 , pp.507 – 512,2016.

[36] Aruna Bhat ,**"K-medoids Clustering Using Partitioning Around Medoids For Performing Face Recognition"** , International Journal of Soft Computing, Mathematics and Control (IJSCMC), Vol. 3, No. 3,pp.1-12, August ,2014.

[37] Kantardzic M, **"Data Mining: Concepts, Models, Methods and Algorithms"**, IEEE International Journal of Data Mining & Knowledge Management Process (IJDKP) ,Vol.3, No.5, September, 2013.

[38] Russ J. C, **"The Image Processing Handbook"** , Five edition, CRC Press; Taylor and Francis Group, ISBN 0-8493-7254-2,2006.

[39] M.A.Massoud,M.Sabee,M.Gergais andR.Bakhit , **"Automated New License Plat Recognition in Egypt"** ,Engineering Journal ,production and hosting by Elsevier, Vol.52,pp.219-326,2013.

[40] Gaurav L. Agrawal and Prof. Hitesh Gupta, **"Optimization of C4.5 Decision Tree Algorithm for Data Mining Application"** , International Journal of Emerging Technology and Advanced Engineering, Vol. 3, Issue .3, March ,2013.

[41] Benjamin Devéze & Matthieu Fouquin, **"DATAMINING C4.5 – DBSCAN"**, SCIA Ecole pour l'informatique et techniques avancées, PROMOTION,2005.

[42] Jitendra Agrawal, Seema Sharma and Sanjeev Sharma, **"Classification Through Machine Learning Technique: C4.5 Algorithm based on Various Entropies"**, International Journal of Computer Applications (0975 – 8887),Vol.82,No.16, November,2013

[43] António Eduardo de Barros Ruano, **" Artificial Neural Networks"** , Centre for Intelligent Systems,University of Algarve,Faro, Portugal .

[44] da Silva, I.N, Hernane Spatti, D, Andrade Flauzino, R, Liboni, L.H.B, dos Reis Alves and S.F, **"Artificial Neural Networks"**,Spring,2017.

[45] Simon Haykan, **" Neural Networks and Learning Machines"** , 3nd Edition, Pearson Education, Inc, Pearson Prentice Hall, pp.1-906,2008.

[46] Prof. Janusz Kacprzyk and Prof. Lakhmi C. Jain **,"Data Mining Concepts ,Models and Techniques"** ,Spring,vol.12. Florin Gorunescu, ISBN 978-3-642-19720-8,2011.

[47] Baiddaa Mutasher Rashed AL—Safy, **" Early Detection and Classification of Melanoma Skin Cancer"** , M.Sc. Thesis,   University of Basra,   College of Science, Department of Computer Science,2015.

[48] ShrishailAyya M. Hiremath, **"Anfis Based Data Rate Prediction For Cognitive Radio"**,M.Sc. Thesis, department of electronics and communication engineering national institute of technology, rourkela, india,2010.

[49] Ben Krose , **"An Introduction to Neural Networks"**, Faculty of Mathematics & Computer Science, Institute of Robotics and System Dynamics, University of Amsterdam, November, 1996.

[50] Ajith Abraham , **"Artificial Neural Networks"**, Handbook of Measuring System Design, edited by Peter H. Sydenham and Richard Thorn, John Wiley & Sons, Ltd. ISBN: 0-470-02143-8,2005.

[51] Anil K. Jain, Jianchange Mao and K. M. Mohiuddin , **"Artificial Neural Networks: A Tutorial",** IEEE ,1996.

[52] R. C. Gonzalez, R. E. Woods and S. L. Eddins, **"Digital Image Processing Using Matlab(R) "** , Prentice Hall, 2004.

[53] C. Solomon and T. Breckon, **"Fundamentals of Digital Image Processing"** , John Wiley & Sons, 2011.

[54] P. K. Ghosh and K. Deguchi, **"Mathematics of Shape Description a Morphological Approach to Image Processing and Computer Graphics"** , JohnWiley & Sons (Asia) Pte Ltd,2008.

[55] P. Soille**, " Morphological Image Analysis"** , Springer-Verlag Berlin Heidelberg ,2004.

[56] Emad M. A , **" Real Time System to Recognition of Iraqi License Plate for Vehicle Tracking"** , M.Sc. Thesis, College of science, Al-Mustansiriyah University , Iraq, 2015.

[57] Wazalwar D.E, **"A Design Flow for Robust License Plate Localization and Recognition in Complex Scenes"** , Journal of Transportation Technologies,2012.

[58] Khalid W. M , **"A Vehicle License Plate Detection and Recognition System"**, Journal of Computer Science, ISSN: 15493636**,** Vol**.** 8**,** Issue. 3**, pp.** 310-315 , 2012.

[59] Michel Marie Deza and Elena Deza , **" Encyclopedia of Distances"** , Springer, pp. 94,2009.

[60] Christopher Clapham, James Nicholson, **" <u>Oxford Concise Dictionary of Mathematics</u>"** , OUP oxford,2009.

[61] A. H. Stroud, **" Approximate Calculation of Multiple Integrals"** , Prentice-Hall Inc., Englewood Cli_s, N. J.,1971.

[62] Dr Yeap Ban Har, Dr Joseph Yeo,Teh Keng Seng , Loh Cheng Yee,Ivy Chow,Neo Chai Meng and Jacinth Liew , **"New Syllabus Mathematics Teacher's Resource Book1"** ,7th edition,OXFORD UNIVERSITY Press,2018.

[63] Dan B. Marghitu and Mihai Dupac, **" Advanced Dynamics"** ,ch2, Springer, New York, NY,pp.73-141,2012.

[64] Hermann K, **"Real-Time Systems Design Principles for Distributed Embedded Applications"** , Second edition,Springer,2011.

[65] Pavol OR.ANSKÝ, **" Fundamentals of Mathematical Statistics"** , Statistics Faculty of Management, University of Presov, Slovakia, 2009.

[66] A. Miranda Neto, A. Correa Victorino, I. Fantoni, D. E. Zampieri, J. V. Ferreira and D. A. Lima, **" Image Processing Using Pearson's Correlation Coefficient: Applications on Autonomous Robotics"** , IEEE , April 2013.

[67]   Rafael C .Gonzalez and Richard E. woods ,**"Digital image processing "** ,prentice hall,2002.

[68]   Wei Dai and Wei Ji , **"A MapReduce Implementation of C4.5 Decision Tree Algorithm"** ,international Journal of Database Theory and Application,Vol.7,No.1,pp.49-60,2014.

[69]   Mariam A.Sheha , Mai S.Mabrouk and Amr Sharawy, **"Automatic Detection of Melanoma Skin Cancer using Texture Analysis"** , International Journal of Computer Applications, Vol. 42, No.20, March, 2012.

[70]   M. Mohandes, S. A-Buraiky, T. Halawani and S. Al-Baiyat , **"Automation of the Arabic sign language recognition"** , International Conference on Information and Communication Technologies: From Theory to Applications, 2004.

[71]   M. A. Mohandes, **" Recognition of Two-Handed Arabic signs using the CyberGlove. Arabian"**, Journal for Science and Engineering, pp.669-677,2013.

[72]   M. Mohandes, and M. Deriche , **"Arabic Sign Language Recognition by Decisions Fusion Using Dempster-Shafer Theory of Evidence"** , In Proceedings Computing, Communications and IT Applications Conference (ComComAp) ,2013.

[73]   K. Assaleh and Al-Rousan, M , **" Recognition of Arabic Sign Language Alphabet Using Polynomial Classifiers"** , EURASIP Journal on Applied Signal Processing (JASP), pp. 2136-2145, 2005.

[74]   M. Maraqa and R. Abu-Zaiter, **"Recognition of Arabic Sign Language (ArSL) Using Recurrent Neural Networks"** , Applications of Digital Information and Web Technologies, 2008.

[75]   Manar Maraqa, Farid Al-Zboun, Mufleh Dhyabat and Raed Abu Zitar, **"Recognition of Arabic sign language (ArSL) Using Recurrent Neural Networks"** , J. Intell. Learn. Syst. Appl, pp. 41-52, 2012.

[76]   T. Shanableh, and K. Assaleh, **"Arabic Sign Language Recognition in User-Independent Mode"** , International Conference on Intelligent and Advanced Systems, ICIAS ,2007.

[77]   T. Shanableh, and K. Assaleh , **"Two Tier Feature Extractions for Recognition of Isolated Arabic Sign Language Using Fisher's Linear Discriminants"** , IEEE International Conference on Acoustics, Speech and Signal Processing, 2007.

[78] M. Mohandes and M. Deriche, **"Image Based Arabic Sign Language Recognition"** , Proceedings of the 8th International Symosium on Signal Processing and its Applications (2005), pp. 86-89, Aug, 2005.

[79] M. Mohandes, M. Deriche, U. Johar and S. Ilyas, **"A Signer-Independent Arabic Sign Language Recognition System Using Face Detection, Geometric Features, and a Hidden Markov Models"** , Computers and Electrical Engineering ,2012.

[80] Prof.reyadh Naoum, Dr.Hussein H. Owaied and Shaimaa Joudeh,**" Development of A New Arabic Sign Language Recognition Using K-nearest neighbor Algorithm"** , Journal of Emerging Trends Computing and Information Sciences , pp. 1173-1178,2012.

[81] F. F. Al Mashagba, E. F. Al Mashagba, and M. O. Nassar, **" Automatic Isolated-Word Arabic Sign Language Recognition System Based on Time Delay Neural Networks: New Improvements"** , Journal of Theoretical and Applied Information Technology , pp. 42-47,2013.

[82] M. M. Zaki, and S. I. Shaheen, **" Sign Language Recognition Using A Combination of New Vision Based Features"** , Pattern Recognition Letters , pp. 572-577,2011.

[83] E. E. Hemayed, and A. S. Hassanien, **"Edge-Based Recognizer for Arabic Sign Language Alphabet (ArS2V-Arabic sign to voice) "** , in Proceedings of International Computer Engineering Conference (ICENCO) ,2010.

[84] Nashwa El-Bendary, Hossam M. Zawbaa, Mahmoud S. Daoud, Aboul Ella Hassanien and Kazumi Nakamatsu , **" ArSLAT: Arabic Sign Language Alphabets Translator"** , International conference on Computer Information Systems and Industrial Management Applications (CISIM) ,2010.

[85] K. Assaleh, T. Shanableh, M. Fanaswala, F. Amin and H. Bajaj, **" Continuous Arabic Sign Language Recognition in User Dependent Mode"** , Journal of Intelligent Learning Systems and Applications , pp. 19-27,2010.

[86] N. R. Albelwi, and Y. M, **"Real-Time Arabic Sign Language (ArSL) Recognition"** ,International Conference on Communications and Information Technology , pp.497-501,2012.

[87] Nada B. Ibrahim, Mazen M. Selim and Hala H. Zayed, **"An Automatic Arabic Sign Language Recognition System (ArSLRS)"** , Journal of King Saud University – Computer and Information Sciences ,2017.

APPENDIX

A

Publications

ACSAT

Date: 16-11-2018

Dr. Shaker K. Ali,
University of Thi-Qar
Iraq

Greetings...

We are delighted to inform you that your article entitled "Convert Gestures of Arabic Numbers into Voice" has been accepted to be presented in the 6th International Conference on Advanced Computer Science Applications and Technologies (ACSAT2018), which will be conducted from the 10th-12th December 2018 in Langkawi / Malaysia.

All accepted papers will be entitled for the publication in a SCOPUS indexed journal. We would like to thank you for your professional cooperation. We are looking forward to work with you in your future research.

Please accept our highest consideration.

Yours Sincerely,

Organizing Committee
ACSAT2018

Ministry of Higher Education &
Scientific Research
University of Thi Qar
A scientific and Refereed Journal
Issued by University of Thi Qar

بسم الله الرحمن الرحيم
جمهورية العراق

وزارة التعليم العالي و البحث العلمي
رئاسة جامعة ذي قار
مجلة جامعة ذي قار
علمية .. فصلية .. محكمة

العدد: ٤٧٧٦
التاريخ: ٢٠١٧/٤/١

الى/ أ.م.د. شاكر كاظم علي المحترم
الباحثة زهور مساعد ايدام المحترمة
جامعة ذي قار/ كلية علوم الحاسوب والرياضيات

<u>م/ قبول نشر</u>

نهديكم أطيب تحياتنا...

تدارست هيئة التحرير البحث المقدم من قبلكم والموسوم بـ
"Gestures conversion to Arabic letters"
وبعد الاطلاع على آراء السادة المقومين فقد تقرر قبول البحث للنشر☑، وسينشر في الاعداد القادمة من المجلة.

أ.د. ضياء غني لفتة
مدير التحرير
٢٠١٣/٩/

نسخة منه الى:
• شعبة المجلة العلمية.
• الصادرة.
م.م. ود 4/8

Address: Iraq - Thi-Qar – Nassiriyah
Tel.: 07821527107
Journal web site: https://jutq.utq.edu.iq
E-mail: Research.develop@utq.edu.iq

العنوان: العراق - ذي قار -- الناصرية
تلفون: 07821527107
الموقع الالكتروني: https://jutq.utq.edu.iq
البريد الالكتروني: Research.develop@utq.edu.iq

APPENDIX

B

Tables of selected results

Letter or number or Word	Feature Geometry																		
	Distance								Slope								Area	Perimeter
	Dist	Dist	Dist	Dist	Dist	Dist	Dist	Dist	SI1	SI2	SI3	SI4	SI5	SI6	SI7	SI8		
ا	0.3284206483940837	0.3291516316327342	0.1591446237228035	0.1659905790935961	0.2326098454780771	0.2108826171099066	0.2053317992667356	0.1924053246460976	-	-	1.1947683630218258	1.1012401577304418	0.5488729604954179	0.3451956152604833	-	-	0.8397	1.252278
ز	0.4534573598515189	0.4527459384060694	0.21099487717127383	0.21333807402205907	0.32417191696959113	0.3241535193331423	0.18259193990904754	0.18732871820040398	0.06422973855402388	-	0.7968494502275058	0.7856751296611861	0.01304254673845189	-	-1.5298319208907374	1.3418072829954353	1.1648	1.3166499999999999
ج	0.4634710619358843	0.4586017560601242	0.2501384081197041	0.2605329017349305	0.3874750805186451	0.3878059083666514	0.1735670595980470	0.1928610352212438	0.1591986175555016	0.0657674892833364	0.6933129558449466	0.6606003742515386	-	-	-	1.1185547282324089	1.6039	1.287304

[illegible]	[illegible]	[illegible]	[illegible]
0.14255848765734	0.145324197500395	0.151429742941880	0.4767653409499911
0.12548500962629	0.085275424659975	0.127528972340934	0.4740177550173368
0.15345734930438	0.153577313491167	0.154727231153943	0.1756455826203421
0.16243430712719	0.159768570981586	0.160816915664584	0.31016484366464625
0.17344683096407	0.161493482962621	0.162168160144060	0.43912504524050716
0.16057022111782	0.151378748105666	0.150624289932764	0.4399614073546689
0.19252122777743	0.185946366000479	0.187479761636447	0.21041569693345474
0.19287638895061	0.184732365374449	0.189749504604709	0.17690074796807723
0.76903799399092	0.947454905994677	0.751094616526329	0.10888328211577068
0.61573363405409	-	0.519774030880042	0.01788198918823604
1.16275571163794	1.317404522956688	1.24642485064066	-1.2184913614998027
1.04949571230772	1.195922191189197	1.14803322086506	0.5603886509957019
0.74447556865363	0.888504821383344	0.802890380266959	-
0.65274301680264	0.832935785892058	0.725953239264291	-
-	-	1.47810394804258	-0.9284316971171078
1.50625591380397	-	1.39053403378647	1.2609336265498392
0.2846	0.2638	0.302300000000000	1.9823
0.567474	0.5370699999999999	0.681550000000000	1.3591220000000002

ن.	ن	ن.	ن
0.3307641705655938	0.3708153979935700	0.207630179139558	0.212392980129824
0.3302378809245104	0.3711020263390532	0.188286438807206	0.195042604230765
0.17976376719345943	0.1829770946568024	0.201129863477789	0.153490454217606
0.1806585541839168	0.2103732606652483	0.207980405435946	0.160554250465852
0.26934852202675846	0.2847377147876228	0.228036799527159	0.162225991995272
0.2733253609229321	0.2855982644258306	0.218880235553938	0.152341143333530
0.17442460098043372	0.1825309011512545	0.184432453200014	0.204975502771072
0.1694828935959617	0.1829470991123401	0.184721580944519	0.212392980129824
0.06982586660337711	0.0363518260440769	0.436045814665028	1.074112388789329
-0.04116236887984478	-	-	1.025230493365739
1.3079473267345116	1.101439243630326	0.834077546630485	1.270119989100577
1.2901290961256957	0.8878482179595479	0.798457185293734	1.150857572365772
-0.21099504830656582	-	0.514947294277343	0.863116166912024
-0.270655527264057	-	0.435338585954739	0.806189196137528
-1.1575773453088647	-	-	1.145658991447872
1.2301424678318245	1.19445318773604746	1.508308641793141	1.074112388789329
1.1072	1.1439	0.505	0.2994
0.929568	1.0573119999999998	0.9553780000000001	0.7454240000000001

ؤ	ئٕ	ئ
0.21776354576228746	0.21829771563628725	0.3598392690443021
0.22307684604933006	0.2189726133460961	0.35847549578675836
0.18096555550003443	0.19253087050280482	0.21536821182821952
0.1722900767507501	0.19120243666544495	0.20854460499637623
0.250721679985393	0.19306035050495032	0.32143111219301074
0.25109445010001596	0.19735853923539196	0.32604351273537013
0.17620383615557286	0.17002787658704202	0.17860103162136298
0.19242711713133626	0.18527361882775814	0.15205486352242495
-	0.02447737806577603	0.0871685906169451
-	-0.0822514382849 5923	0.00370172436440981
-1.1292223030702548	-1.3531922055121448	-1.0067407545101867
-1.2519703448994157	-1.3872435922463582	-1.0607982940291503
-	-0.21935251978477863	-
-0.118663922747	-0.30187129722641165	-0.2626696313137434
1.2988002091434414	1.0251992529517537	-1.0108631327772901
1.08014751146344	0.9018517293136962	-1.472910268409658
0.8734	0.5445	1.4101
0.779882	1.218906	1.125784

ع	ط	ظ	غ
0.19073870195481	0.194833142909825	0.19099736385825114	0.3048875103561104
0.14547698211850	0.173892462078955	0.11531482429474137	0.30799145965914954
0.15280284607425	0.165137823838885	0.15621034684405766	0.16977008453820427
0.15684751902826	0.173114626965139	0.15684430885558817	0.15300716782968588
0.14802821500403	0.168651488276226	0.1275615934556267	0.2632930444208558
0.12749218951831	0.152646700162933	0.10394981885127659	0.26251183240008996
0.19246816215047	0.176721254038796	0.18103913989462928	0.18808461499046675
0.19742960864677	0.174883814013664	0.19269837613388893	0.19308046083002106
1.02077362833801	0.946730625272058	1.1430817849985717	-
0.81573358459651	0.857000962480172	0.8134086151206862	-
1.30390293897008	1.287552597812358	1.565830170522382	-1.0283999611729309
1.22181224641929	1.157773817810008	1.4807185066252442	-1.2542186332573657
0.65972281708013	0.964146262312664	0.8155173443579252	0.08392278631353041
0.40920133775549	0.889378841182173	0.5713005053917225	0.03328854921703220
1.30961036518394	-	-1.3624732522990992	1.5301991746876094
1.22796450837710	-	1.165998850450039	1.3392946266066756
0.3204	0.2956	0.2866	0.9537
0.6252620000000001	0.8209839999999999	0.8515779999999998	0.9204459999999999

ك	ق	ف	ع
0.43423476023430446	0.272761709524020	0.242467852760338	0.2828407041507
0.4332171538367127	0.274193181074118	0.237422683146968	0.2724616251447
0.17642837835885244	0.183378710955213	0.180684044735447	0.2145815712012
0.17785491423399952	0.180207289529793	0.176298691159737	0.2191275044698
0.39420857062703407	0.277715395150975	0.240161072672657	0.2437689002399
0.3976075489343388	0.278410324496261	0.240086809226275	0.2421994955687
0.22669664841004428	0.161486631687293	0.173014598743558	0.2774087102391
0.2313128532649901	0.179470349095032	0.180048534855712	0.2958968548505
0.06999739517111328	0.028074847412026	0.220295566703267	0.4436234167641
-	-	0.082859707920291	0.3551086533109
1.5320819905954575	-	-	0.8317561012403
1.4383054821781192	-	-	0.8092675904997
-	-	0.029219533887327	0.1451842650906
-0.1439474876929358	-	0.015341147820346	0.0906854317157
-0.7652528047546004	1.492355110075151	1.551867453404267	0.6813921787039
0.7462567030526147	1.113000353539043	1.289732730635612	0.6317021214928
1.902	0.9937	0.8254	0.8146
1.2588519999999999	0.947684	0.8373299999999999	0.981996

ط	د	م	ج
0.2284265338999430	0.23827457115666	0.379469363934079	0.29819456027376406
0.2268842697718816	0.23089467592289	0.372444053433897	0.29092771085885366
0.1671779991505240	0.17534186526785	0.188495735231668	0.24560075820808994
0.1674421218954381	0.18438980302198	0.186603757776400	0.23921933584400368
0.2370595074795061	0.18476686213477	0.312216267167137	0.2236671439583887
0.2382055835471761	0.17848167159392	0.316681033160465	0.22454003349555823
0.1750862432388517	0.18392559431524	0.167556847010794	0.14676824642192748
0.1879754491341615	0.20990989065538	0.154630042419685	0.15117448239338893
0.1171697986355313	0.61003924334278	0.255500144288859	0.3541209305738307
-	0.56269114068711	0.168798058987692	0.27882307094351955
-	1.15158777163971	-	-0.862935407596723
1.472256591571022	1.05235101494796	-	-0.8947004923619165
-	0.42882143682337	-	-
-	0.34379373296589	-	-0.08950393355111011
1.260104058875648	1.22718507346108	-	1.550181260211808
1.0904533992295264	0.97018887619717	1.305897188511710	1.3279065764571623
0.9097	0.5756	1.2731	0.6582
0.9661719999999999	1.036228	1.146906	1.00409

1	صفر	ي	و
0.451499092917143	0.213614554323827	0.2540912082415813	0.117089242079016
0.454837409796415	0.213752710905687	0.24132843441203547	0.105577205862504
0.183122811331653	0.180433074052829	0.2640287540359894	0.178479852000769
0.184406156524838	0.179079851452837	0.25457745225844036	0.176232984413724
0.322826330493761	0.204924552021437	0.19632414312390573	0.180967344601080
0.322429917877639	0.206911272929681	0.19968136899373087	0.193379115088649
0.235372849393488	0.157482959269623	0.1991754501137132	0.158414717487148
0.212695247818600	0.169550146580858	0.2533469679318218	0.157953393947432
-	0.0656603957890000	0.6176908361038919	0.515509105772609
-	-0.0748481464336550	0.5387879721212017	0.265694477108445
1.18396986446404	-1.34826802408710	-0.7649596784562157	-
1.16722866266479	-1.38458541771596	-0.8012372998294855	1.486751015357134
0.050384946172233	-0.117463996398481	-	-
0.009073019323606	-0.181503565659500	-	-
-	1.52958924898234	0.8565264101116571	-
-	1.18911513843423	0.6360378809668422	1.516708389253993
1.25870000000000	0.711000000000000	0.6384	0.3983
1.22073000000000	0.791892000000000	1.094792	0.6060399999999999

5	4	3	2
0.20367631292233	0.248044543655645	0.307349251715921	0.415491658061348
0.20160443866246	0.247775591043030	0.300049510637893	0.407542269985562
0.19029784273436	0.221629423814922	0.241432827178945	0.407232658619454
0.18473951220696	0.215750265248856	0.233523107501850	0.392314549518238
0.18324632446547	0.213732992533910	0.256811903814375	0.355303330188624
0.18103779337636	0.218942392165286	0.255865641643589	0.354772394964296
0.16400321463978	0.161208434705372	0.150474312261906	0.275987073626563
0.16667501061517	0.239246507479863	0.142348609913385	0.158648113823126
0.14614307445126	0.058588366899326	0.293432344800936	0.247488028944366
0.03138693595068	-0.03556031502916	0.197575736888035	0.152185026783999
-	-	-	-0.452961362192143
-	-	-	-0.471554239980217
0.35487566624693	-	0.294065392229309	0.164594563196081
0.32033863686200	-	0.281596631335961	0.155325719214079
1.45976680412697	-	-1.23825905038389	-0.582320032172222
1.36022321061932	0.547418823023426	-1.53012539027194	1.27553294121802
0.48290000000000	0.7097	0.775100000000000	1.41050000000000
1.18683600000000	1.338328	1.30276600000000	1.55243400000000

9	8	7	6
0.16955338618981403	0.165641964255776	0.2402355723682763	0.32229184306382075
0.17139411788473802	0.165874044365345	0.2510199280827898	0.32170222362728346
0.19068354113803185	0.203826455860175	0.2483011569280417	0.18112647796700299
0.19468728328997925	0.207573080574774	0.2431457335432409	0.18222540404280813
0.18368509775330352	0.097881726277036	0.1697748213165143	0.2477230257819788
0.18109231907645332	0.103120271351776	0.1686277252104180	0.2490358842173 6292
0.14727044905769748	0.136029914683377	0.2124645678505362	0.1539176592895091
0.1543533496886018	0.137327218166177	0.2200696444246317	0.15283482722023473
-	0.036382777035611	-	0.06051871850062397
-	-	-	-
1.3704139457901385	1.317215519326569	-	1.4880810820097312
1.2864208062988156	1.254995172333562	-	1.4333643149083442
0.8969340526584489	0.040619513100293	0.1922999791264466	-
0.8854477859346855	-	0.1534841481186389	-0.4109842866955584
1.4661793233813194	-	0.9893762474677443	-1.4516316088030525
1.2497188904069678	1.432982937116281	0.9387231289330501	-1.560121138579401
0.3906	0.3375	0.4939	0.9102
0.9453299999999999	0.7769819999999998	0.848414	0.972626

أحبك حقاً – I love you	تمنى لك حياة سعيدة I hope for you happy life	10
0.2712372220004733	0.239502918071322	0.0960929126656852
0.2715646689025912	0.241678925508596	0.0656431682534338
0.2175992051492526	0.215803470815530	0.2100535917596194
0.2143808326269026	0.214379767184299	0.2095323968515139
0.2039722289891700 6	0.217295129070760	0.0954001601585802
0.2093488270833407	0.218297446199608	0.0957073712244605
0.16805821993905828	0.142255745975282	0.1278250995732202
0.21427853902426625	0.189007595956426	0.1341037727416159
0.02048730164568303	-0.0675929389381310	0.875829396818651
-	-0.150252487143022	-
-1.221288713259514	-1.40496737528946	-
-1.265128568209072	-1.45098991407273	-
-	-0.298114700216040	-
-0.318502743743946	-0.312711387700739	-
0.8740524611172139	1.01031185460498	-
0.6453851539294351	0.691234907517983	1.1763631531850958
0.6271	0.662200000000000	0.2564
1.023948	1.00358600000000	0.580116

أنت you	ألم Pain	أنا بخير Im ok	اريد التحدث معك I want talk with you
0.163150350659500	0.2835657535400354	0.282837449322198	0.2302829481673717
0.163149456669576	0.2885547029757713	0.2779768948925992	0.21680430116723456
0.167405217572744	0.2650195531517218	0.2162818028545709	0.15218615940089243
0.170167044292297	0.2500453364219794	0.2229704667877631	0.15829889462693772
0.201970202373481	0.3039101185548659	0.2365332278456756	0.15532943670530572
0.169290453390613	0.3039950513882322	0.2267576024062726	0.14813140326890054
0.170698160198269	0.1628608519166721	0.1719707936720187	0.2194866701936344
0.168409810547312	0.2373850389042202	0.1705251545873323	0.2302829481673717
0.133216141341615	-	0.3242423866265796	0.963578575413429
-	-	0.2673789443470979	0.9197012243490219
1.400958884797067	-	0.855168992995985	1.2457292295099494
1.323654876472777	-	0.8213158114140018	1.1457907997768115
0.585804798116185	-	0.5479732093105253	0.8261313432519087
0.108487943037677	-	0.4726160395709266	0.7803637240176365
-	1.5330209592061705	-	1.0384812672297061
-	0.7553898719971308	-	0.963578575413429
0.5942	1.3624	0.5302	0.2598
1.2483759999999997	1.076596	0.9885779999999998	0.6816120000000001

هذا رهيب This is terrible	اعتذار Apology	عمل جيد Good job	موافق agree
0.4335572840830563	0.489121559251914	0.141799717483062	0.32278502496735084
0.4364099792463138	0.491325676073379	0.146213473216936	0.3255675054637184
0.19277691955750198	0.156706161047307	0.179801835478444	0.16878755008726287
0.1697554521670143	0.149759437043914	0.168469688171556	0.16942304792524912
0.36059662706037626	0.364916039611008	0.169498056093562	0.243907405562578
0.3607254795266057	0.364018254616953	0.164095443010730	0.24626545699871794
0.2767370234816539	0.196902298566015	0.174422552070851	0.18430389538547515
0.3449449233115856	0.206098004941935	0.177198266258073	0.16822350604324682
-0.06084269910409808	-	0.068552550669225	0.01240628102754519
-0.12951215635914504	-	-	-
-0.9460406323508254	-	-	1.388657015568819
-1.1709082513786777	-	1.257843389643752	1.3693066412574133
-	0.144135160691922	0.301215456586944	-
-	0.126009976510206	0.165003010050202	-
0.6938358891970106	1.406518992560657	-	-1.1383541236873547
0.538723575223552	1.230091485745085	1.353898216737493	-1.4681344794703879
1.3886	1.2289	0.7233	1.0989
1.4382120000000003	1.266214	0.7337119999999999	1.3655840000000001

رئيس جمهورية the Republic's president	قف Stop	الم كثير Big pain	الم قليل Little pain
0.2606937171284699	0.250720473541643	0.24592115148	0.17122619226
0.2646126909150731	0.250336002613837	0.21329346077	0.16062399108
0.1372703126230572	0.222124515834009	0.17393015798	0.17540845495
0.1372430481302036	0.221516743463072	0.17997094202	0.18051582059
0.1684644963742860	0.220569851023561	0.19768112179	0.19914430918
0.1693470479404372	0.226223416476191	0.19447514389	0.18781421124
0.2092851039881431	0.132349777034583	0.19237874191	0.19631313931
0.2129243896635999	0.112517568223685	0.19293987021	0.20194488054
-	0.0630390001695503	0.63415059417	0.53338216811
-	-0.0301186051629393	0.37962188780	0.40796551021
-	-1.46454881245365	0.94490313663	1.05908828137
1.4868590514246571	-1.49447911636285	0.89985617831	1.01076848397
-	-0.193716888105320	0.51652248465	0.64425682374
-	-0.295104135058338	0.48670991187	0.55901135538
1.2204725747648022	-1.01546998813161	1.56330412168	1.16529468295
1.176345805736952	1.53918888079243	1.49414478383	1.10458707543
0.4614	0.679500000000000	0.4349	0.4164
0.8195659999999999	0.854660000000000	0.851104	0.81647

اقتباس quotation	سؤال question	ملكي royal	وقوف stand
0.30622434458287516	0.3557821355197502	0.17107629323904	0.26689966827654
0.3183671128553041	0.3555204339992590	0.17550109117567	0.25429609065587
0.2305504109204317	0.1563385342143119	0.19909173480913	0.18063948667909
0.2474689981174275	0.2049974176670604	0.20393006398839	0.16549496155315
0.2902060001747766	0.2615877118511481	0.14694820466131	0.25186454393385
0.2931976141619229	0.2628413278656298	0.13643971384205	0.25984797274209
0.1776506158160764	0.1799217468005843	0.14937925846729	0.24731146472187
0.1689411236166929	0.1796277166727378	0.15025616188027	0.26689966827654
0.2270506530258075	0.0627955709346766	-	0.71123115956182
-	-	-	0.65161500798264
0.7938807845378338	1.4107215956602526	1.23046590671282	-
0.7265952637894122	0.8524370426246174	1.16879494639955	-
-	0.0038475575164070	0.72705796861054	-
-0.320128474996279	-	0.63566544041042	-
-	-1.469174951358129	-	0.78167481397882
1.5607435919996595	1.4867410124620883	1.32283703747193	0.71123115956182
1.2332	1.0714	0.44100000000000	0.61970000000000
1.2778720000000001	1.046198	0.66996800000000	1.08808000000000

APPENDIX

C

Data base images

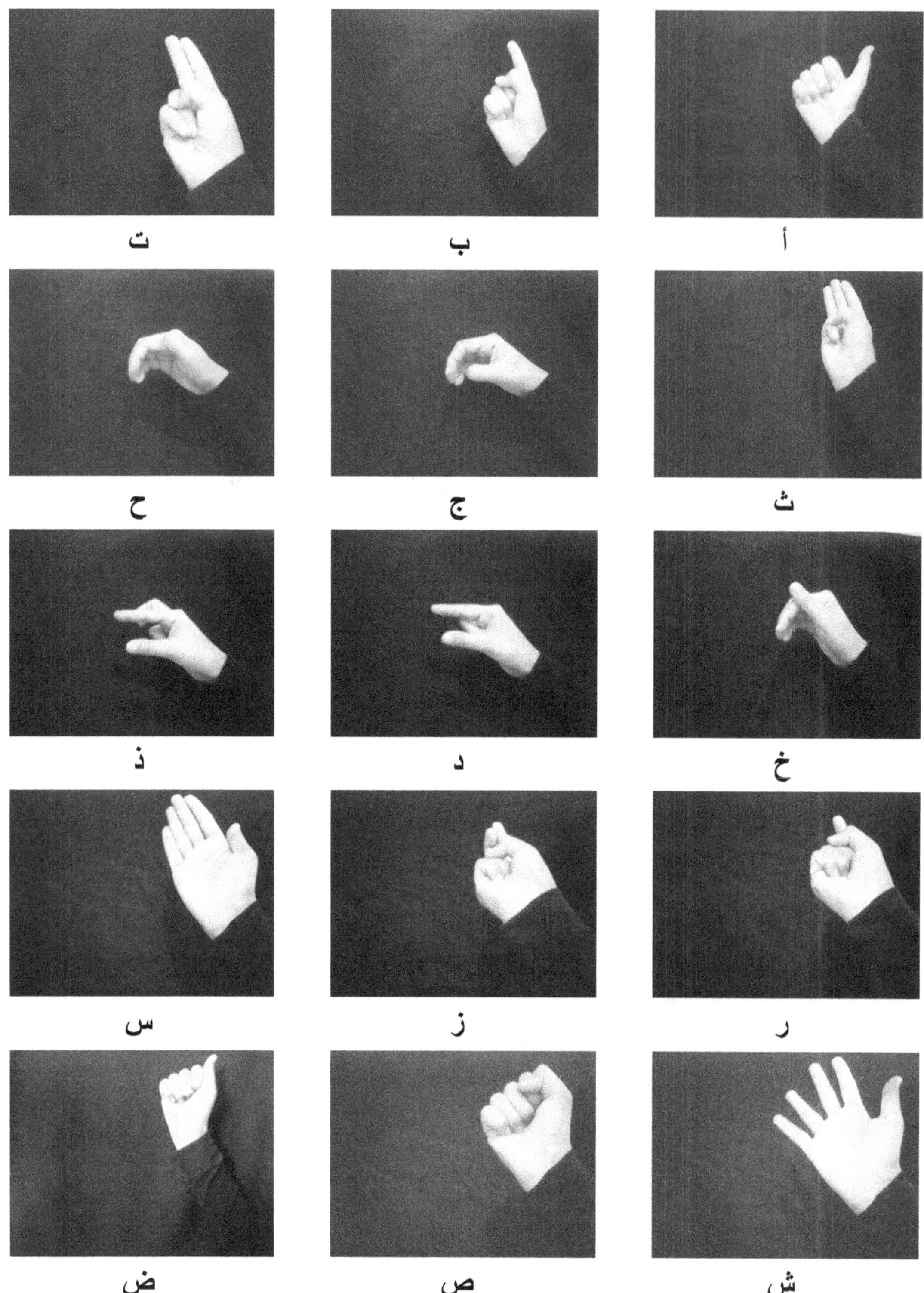

ت
ب
أ
ح
ج
ث
ذ
د
خ
س
ز
ر
ض
ص
ش

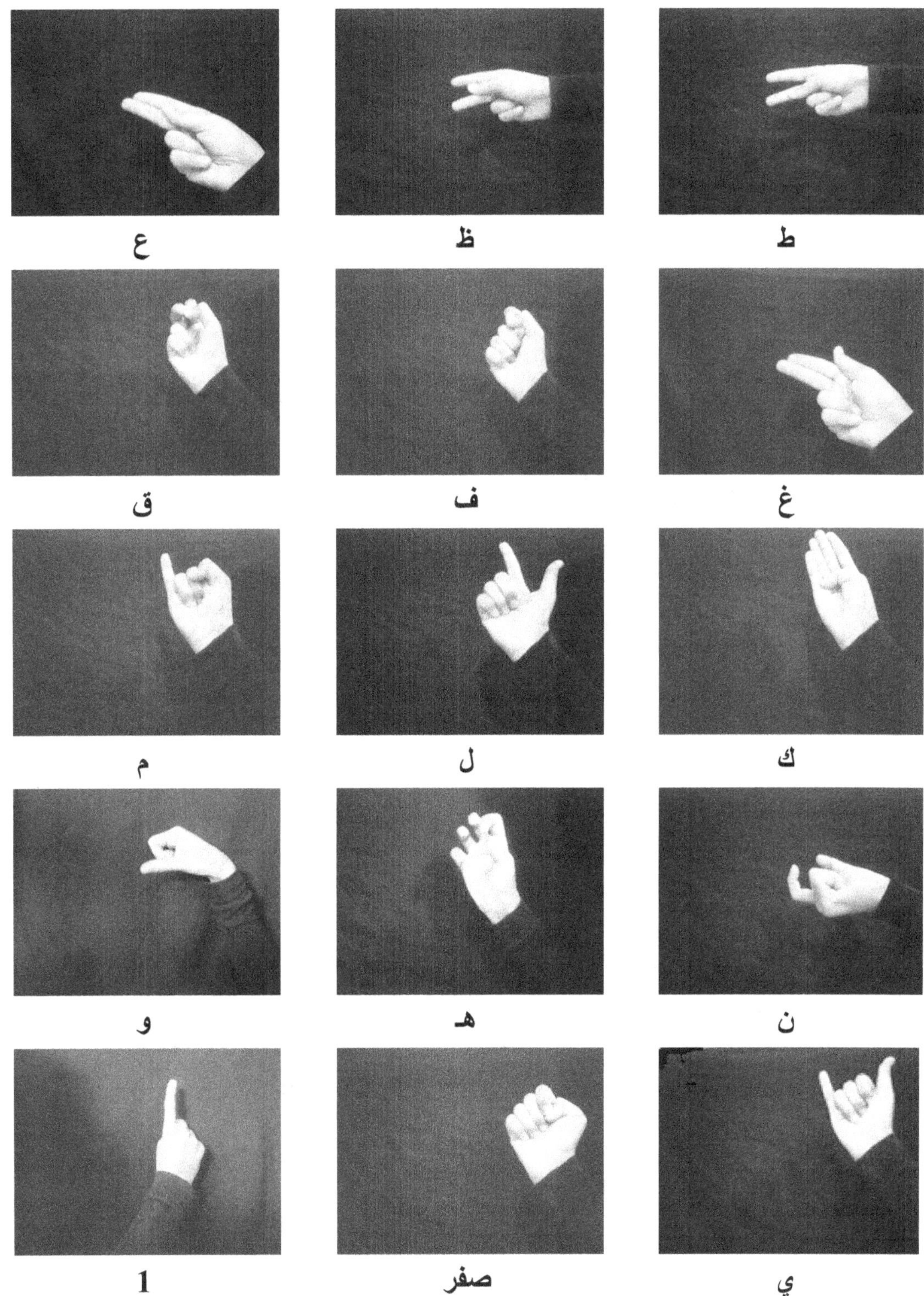

ع
ظ
ط
ق
ف
غ
م
ل
ك
و
هـ
ن
1
صفر
ي

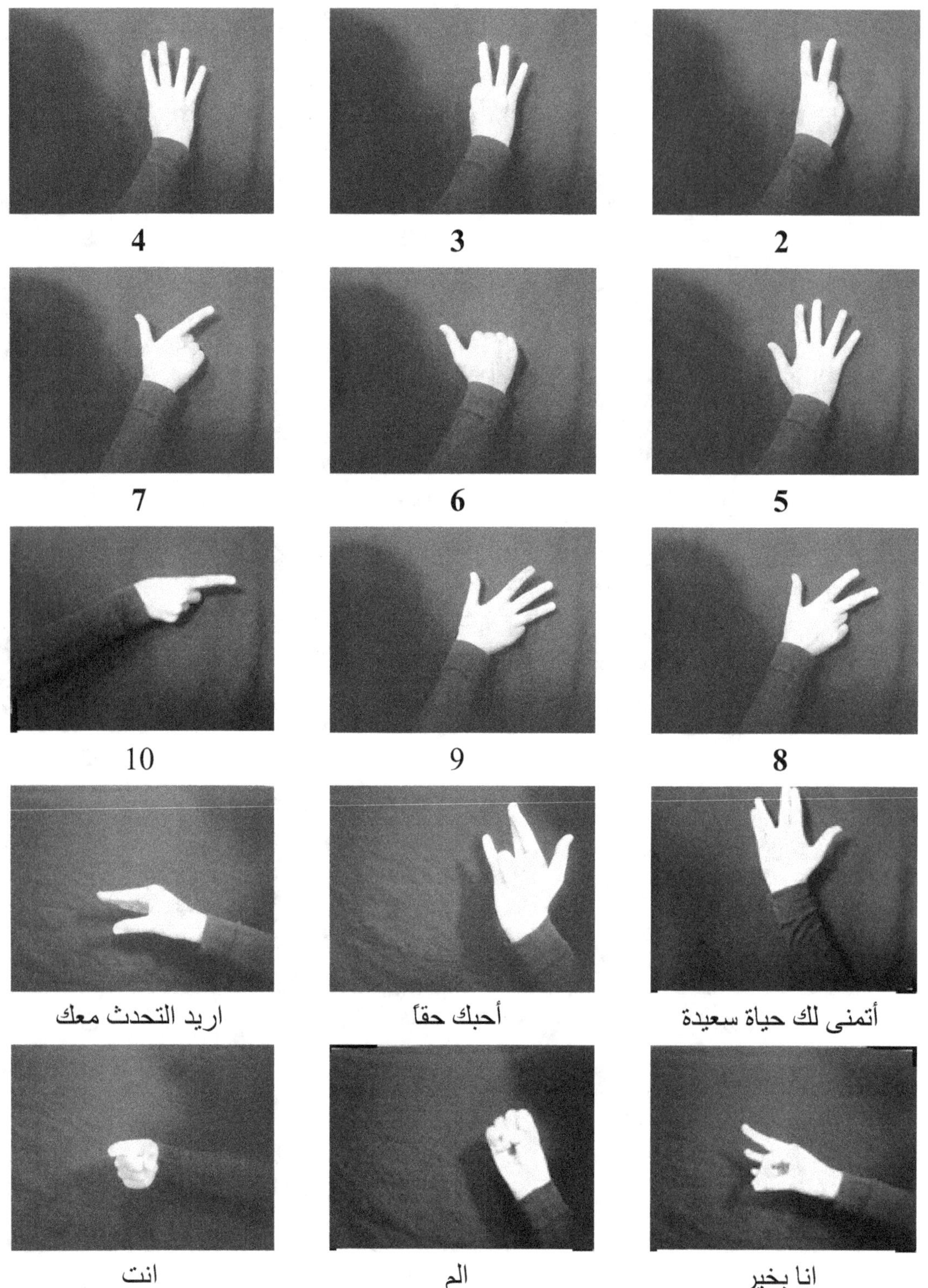

2	**3**	**4**
5	**6**	**7**
8	**9**	**10**
أتمنى لك حياة سعيدة	أحبك حقاً	اريد التحدث معك
انا بخير	الم	انت

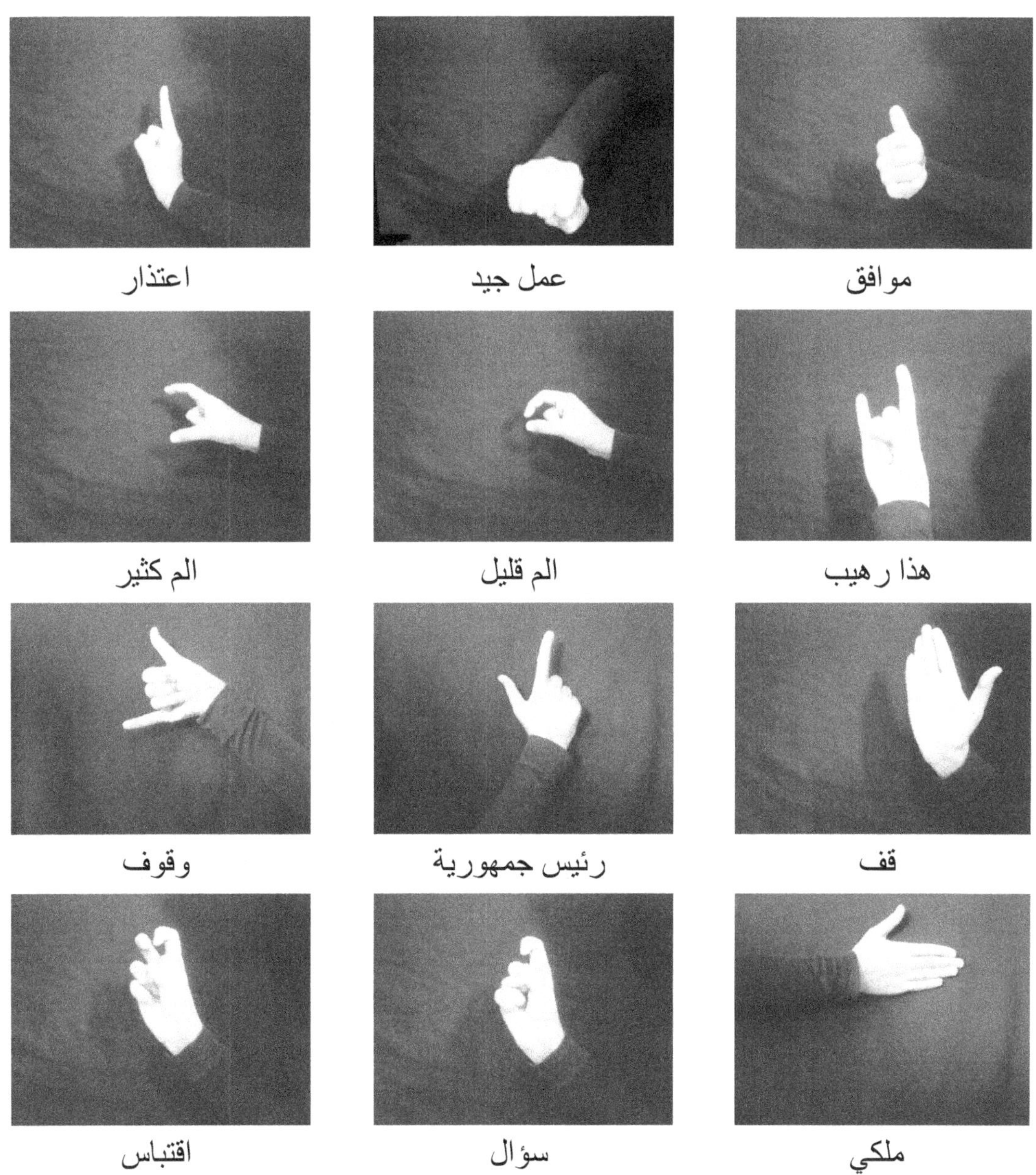

اعتذار
عمل جيد
موافق
الم كثير
الم قليل
هذا رهيب
وقوف
رئيس جمهورية
قف
اقتباس
سؤال
ملكي

المستخلص

التواصل وهو وسيلة للتعبير عن الآراء او الافكار وذلك من خلال التواصل اللفظي او غير اللفظي ويكون التواصل اللفظي بين الاشخاص العاديين   من خلال التحدث. اما الاشخاص البكم الذين لا يستطيعون التحدث فيكون التواصل بينهم ومع الناس الذين يستطيعون التحدث من خلال التواصل غير اللفظي اي من خلال الايماءات ,واما الشخص الاعمى هو الشخص الذي لا يستطيع الرؤية لكن يمكنه السماع اي انه يستطيع ان يتواصل مع الناس من خلال التحدث معهم. وفي هذه الرسالة تم اقتراح خوارزمية للتواصل بين الشخص الابكم والشخص الاعمى وذلك عن طريق اشارة اليد   للشخص الابكم وتحويلها الى صوت لكي يتواصل بين البكم (من خلال الاشارات) والاعمى (سماع صوت التي تمثل الاشارة). وذلك لان الإيماءات هي واحدة من أفضل الطرق للتواصل بين الابكم والاعمى وذلك عن طريق استخدام لغة الإشارة (للابكم) التي تحول الى صوت يستطيع الاعمى سماعه والتواصل فيما بينهم.

تتكون الخوارزمية المقترحة من جزأين ؛ الجزء الأول مخصص لتدريب الخوارزمية اما الجزء الثاني فيقوم باختبار الخوارزمية ، تشمل الخوارزمية عدد من المراحل تبدء بمرحلة الحصول على الفيديو آو الصور يتم تحويل الفيديو إلى صور ثم إجراء معالجة للصور عن طريق تحويل الصور إلى التدرج الرمادي ثم إلى صور ثنائية و من ثم نعمل ترقيع للصور الناتجة باستخدام (Morphology) , الصور الناتجة سوف تكون بمثابة قناع يستخدم لقطع راحة اليد فقط وحذف الخلفية , يتم اجراء عملية الضرب بين القناع والصورة الاصلية (التدرج الرمادي) ستكون النتيجة صورة تحتوي فقط على شكل الاشارة و خلفية سوداء . بعدها يتم تدوير الصورة ومن ثم تحول الى صورة ثنائية ويتم صنع قناع جديد يضرب بالصورة الناتجة من عملية التدوير وتوحيد حجم الصور وبعدها يتم تحويلها الى صوره ثنائية , يتم حساب الصفات من صورة الناتجة حيث يتم حساب الميزات الهندسة (18 ميزه) . ومن ثم يتم تصنيفها باستخدام احدى الخوارزميات (K-mean ،K- medoid ، C4.5، ANN) وبناء قاعدة بيانات لمرحلة الاختبار حيث يكون في الجزء الخاص بالاختبار يتم تكرار نفس الخطوات في مرحلة التدريب ولكن التصنيف سيكون باستخدام ثلاث طرائق (المسافة الإقليدية ، تعديل المسافة الإقليدية المعيارية والارتباط).

النتيجة من استخدام 4.خوارزميات(K-mean يعطي 97.7930٪ ، k-medoid يعطي 97.3620٪ ، C4.5 يعطي 99.8664٪ و ANN يعطي 96.5386٪) أثناء اختبار الحالة (تعديل المسافة الإقليدية القياسية يعطي(98.2456 ٪ &ms3)، كفاءة الارتباط يعطي(96.4912 ٪&ms4)و المسافة الاقليدية يعطي(94.7368 ٪& ms2)).

جمهورية العراق

وزارة التعليم العالي والبحث العلمي

جامعة ذي قار

كلية التربية للعلوم الصرفة

قسم علوم الحاسبات

تميز إشارة اليد للتواصل الاجتماعي بين الاخرس والاعمى

رسالة

مقدمة الى مجلس كلية التربية للعلوم الصرفة في جامعة ذي قار كجزء من متطلبات نيل شهادة الماجستير في علوم الحاسبات

من قبل

زهور مساعد ايدام

بإشراف

أ.م.د شاكر كاظم علي الشريفي

2019   1440

Republic of Iraq

109

Ministry of Higher Education
and Scientific Research
Thi-Qar University
College of Education for pure science
Department of Computer Science

Hand Gesture Recognition for Dumb and Blind Social Communication

A thesis
Submitted to the Council of the College of Education for Pure
Science, University of Thi-Qar in Partial Fulfillment of the
Requirements for the Degree of Master of Science
in Computer Science

By
Zahoor Mosaad Aydam

Supervised By

Assist. Prof. Dr. Shaker Kadhem Ali Al-Sharify

2019   1440

Thank you

www.ingramcontent.com/pod-product-compliance
Lightning Source LLC
Chambersburg PA
CBHW081435250726
48662CB00009B/2806